You Rock!

♥ Michelle
Mio

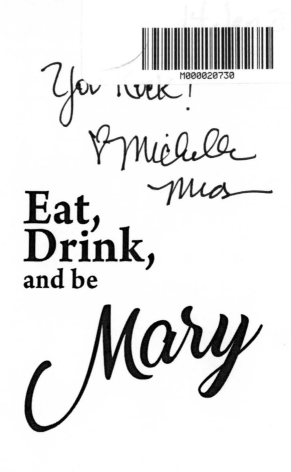

Eat,
Drink,
and be

Mary

14 Jan 2017

Eat,
Drink,
and be

Mary

*a glimpse
into a life
well lived*

Michelle Mras *&* Tony Mras

Vertex Learning, LLC

Washington DC • Atlanta • Denver • St. Louis • Dayton

www.vertexlearning.com

Eat, Drink & Be Mary: A Glimpse into a Life Well Lived

Vertex Learning, LLC Educational Research, Publishing, and Consulting

Copyright © 2016 by Michelle Mras and Tony Mras
Published by Vertex Learning, LLC, Hyattsville, MD 20875 USA

For more information on Vertex Learning Educational Research, Publishing and Consulting, visit our website at www.vertexlearning.com.

ISBN: 978-1-4951-9763-5

Library of Congress Cataloging-in-Publication Data

Mras, Michelle, Mras, Tony

Eat, Drink & Be Mary: A Glimpse into a Life Well Lived

Printed and bound in the United States of America.

Discounts on this title may be available at the author's discretion available in bulk orders: Contact Vertex Learning at info@vertexlearning.com or 240 640 1212.

Eat, Drink & Be Mary

This book is dedicated to
Mary Mras
(Nov 24, 1942 - Sept 18, 2001)

Wife

Mother

Sister

Daughter

Educator

Mentor

Singer

Pianist

Lover of Life

Joy personified

Mentor

Friend

Fighter

Inspiration

"Love is essentially one spirit in two physical entities."

— Aristotle

Mary and I were one. We supported each other's efforts to improve, making the one "we" better. - Tony

Michael and I are one. Accenting each other to make our "we" better. We learned this through example from the strong relationship between his parents. Thank you, Mary and Tony, for raising a phenomenal man to share my life with. - Michelle

Cover Photo: Mary leading her children, Jessica, Michael and Leslie.

Cover photo by KerriGDesign.com

Thank you

Thank you to Mary's children, Jessica, Michael and Leslie for sharing stories of their mother. A special, "thank you" to her loving husband and love of her life, Tony, who not only shares author credit of this book, but for granting me permission to share a brief glimpse at life with Mary, and offered his personal and intimate emails during her final months of battling Leukemia.

A special 'thank you' to Chris and Margaret Hache for correcting my use of the English language. To my amazing husband and children — What would I do without your love and support? I love you with all my heart and soul.

Contents

Chapter *1*

Sometimes there are people who enter your life so quietly that you never realize their significance until they are gone.

Life as the child of a military family has always been an adventure. The multiple moves across states or countries, new schools, and the constant losing and gaining of friends and schools can create extremely introverted or extroverted personalities. I happen to belong to the later category. I was raised the fourth of six children at Clark Air Force Base, Philippines. My father was a United States Air Force Chief Master Sergeant from New Orleans, Louisiana and my mother, a native of the Philippines, worked a government service job. The combination of cultural traits and the number of siblings that I have makes me quiet fearless and sociable. I had no interest in boys like all the other girls my age. That is until August 1983. I was 14 years old attending my sophomore year at Wagner High School, Clark Air Base, Philippines Islands.

My friends and I were sitting on picnic tables waiting for our first day of cross country practice to begin. The day was thick with humidity and the sun was warm and bright. There was a gentle breeze ruffling through the leaves high in the trees that formed a canopy over the eating area.

My attention was captured by a vision in white tennis shoes, tube socks pulled up to just below his knees, white shorts, a pin-striped long sleeve shirt with a burgundy sock tie. A new boy to the school, he was beautiful in his awkwardness. His large brown eyes grew larger when he saw people he knew. His smile lit up the area around him. He wasn't like the rest of the Department of Defense, DoD, school teenagers. The student population was a mix of mostly Air Force and military contractor children. The school dress code was we had to have something on our feet — flip flops. This gangly guy was wearing shoes with socks!

His long gait carried him to the other side of the lunch area to a group of teens that I didn't know well. He put his arm around a girl and he moved smoothly into their fold. Sigh. He was already claimed.

I began to rationalize to myself all the reasons he wouldn't be interested in me even if he was available. He is my polar opposite. He's was tall, I was only 4'10". My hair, when braided, reached my hips. My mixed heritage made me the color of hot chocolate with chestnut brown eyes and a muscular build. He could never find someone like me interesting. I resolved to keep my distance and remain hopeful that his vibrant smile would be flashed my direction on occasion.

The next day, I was sitting in the window of my math class waiting for the teacher to arrive, when a vision came back into my line of sight. This time, I saw the new boy sitting under a palm tree reading a book. His golden tan skin, dark hair and large brown eyes were stunning. I could see him as a handsome 20-year-old. His body would fill out and be gorgeous. But, for now, he was pretty darn cute at 16!

I was smitten, and curious. My friends took it upon themselves to do some snooping for me and discovered his name was Michael. He had a last name that started with an "M", but was missing some vowels. He was a Junior. His family had just moved from Arkansas. His father was an Air Force Colonel. Unfortunately, he was definitely dating the girl I saw him put his arm around.

As I stared at him, a woman approached me from behind.

"What are you looking at?"

"His name is Michael," I said as I pointed, "and he's new to the school."

"He's a cutie!" she sang into my ear, "It's time for class, please find your chair".

The woman sauntered up to the chalk board and wrote her name — Mary M R A S. She turned to the class displaying the same brilliant smile I saw Michael give to his girlfriend, then she winked at me.

"Good afternoon. My name is Mrs. Mah-Rass. No, I am not missing any vowels, my husband is Hungarian."

If I had a shell, I would have climbed back into it. The teacher was Michael's MOTHER! Apparently, she didn't mind that I had an obvious crush on her son. I think that she enjoyed asking me to solve all the hard math questions in front of the class to test if I was smart enough to be worthy of her son.

There was an air of confidence that emanated from Mary. She was a petite woman with birdlike features, short chestnut brown hair, large brown eyes that reminded me of a doll and a dazzling smile that spread from ear to ear. Mrs. Mras informed the class that she was to remain our substitute teacher while our primary teacher was out ill. She was fun to learn from. She kept us anticipating what she would do next. Especially when, to keep the attention of the class, she would breakout into another language in the middle of explaining a math problem. If the class got out of hand, she'd simply state in an acquired Southern belle accent, "Ya'll hush". Little did I know, but her temporary presence in my school life was the beginning of a long friendship. My life would never be the same again.

The softer side of criticism:
When asked by her eldest daughter if she enjoyed
her singing,
Mary responded, "You sing like your Aunt".
Years later, her daughter heard her Aunt sing. It
was not a compliment.

Weeks passed and I still had not spoken to Michael. The cross country team went to Manila to run a meet. It was a muggy 120 degree day and the race was held on city pavement. At some point the route was altered by the all boy school that hosted the meet. The women's race was double the length we set out to run; our two mile race became four miles. Our running paces were off and as each female racer crossed the finish line, we were collapsing. The boys, who had already raced, tried hard to keep us moving. As I crossed the finish line, Michael caught me, kept me walking and gave me sips of water. He was my knight in shining running gear. Bonus... he had his arm around me as he gave me water. Even better, we started talking.

How do you know if you don't try?

Mary shared a story with us after our math lesson was completed. I can't remember what brought us to the topic, possibly because we were all overseas and she was emphasizing the benefit of families staying together. She explained that her husband flew C-130 airplanes during the Vietnam War. They were a young couple and their children were young. He was stationed in Taiwan and flew into Vietnam everyday. She said that worrying about his safety every moment of the day while he was away wasn't worth the stress. She knew her husband was good at what he did. She trusted that he and his crew were well trained. But, not hearing from him made her less productive. She took the initiative to save her teaching dollars and volunteered for substitute teaching work to save every penny she earned. She saved the money to move herself and the children to Taiwan. She found a home in a mostly military community outside of the base. Her tenacity and strong planning made it possible for the family to stay together despite the time of war separating them.

Mary showed me that day, that where there is a will, there is a way. She endeared herself into my memory of a woman I wanted to emulate.

Michael was a Junior, so I didn't have classes with him. But, we did run cross country together. I began dating another boy who was super cute, but avoided Michael. Walking down the school hallway between classes one afternoon, Michael crossed our path.

"I have a strange feeling I'm going to marry that boy one day." I remarked to my friends.

"Maybe you should let him know you like him," one friend remarked, "kinda hard to marry someone you don't talk to."

"He just seems so familiar, like I've always known him." I responded a bit puzzled.

Approaching him was out of the question. My mother taught me well. Good girls don't seek the attention of boys.

You snooze, you lose.

Months passed. My friends kept my secret. With cross country over, I didn't see Michael after school anymore. Soccer season started and I began attending practices to join the soccer team. I befriended a petite green-eyed girl named Leslie who had wild, curly, blonde, shoulder length hair. She was a fabulous player. I loved watching her run with the ball down the field. We became instant friends. One day after practice, I waited for her mother to pick her up in front of the school. I walked home everyday, so I had time to hang out and learn more about my new friend. As we sat on a bench waiting, my crush, Michael, drove up on his red and white Honda Passport. My heart fluttered that he was going to say hello to me.

In my mind's eye he slowly lifted the helmet off his head as if he were in a romance novel, shook his nonexistent military cut hair and said,

"Hey bum, you waiting for mom?"

"Move along no one asked for your input." Leslie yelled, then under her breath, "He's such a butt head".

Michael put his helmet back on and zoomed away while waving his hand.

My thoughts were going in a million directions at once.

"That's your brother?" I gasped in agony.

"Yes, he's my stupid big brother." Leslie replied.

"Oh, you don't look anything alike."

"I look more like my dad."

In case you aren't aware of the mindset of teenage girls, it is a major "no no" to date your friend's brother. We chatted a bit more but, because of my shock that she was Michael's sister, I can only recall a light-headed feeling and that I might have been experiencing heat exhaustion.

Mary arrived to pickup Leslie. I would have never put them together as related. The blonde hair and green eyes on Leslie threw me a curve ball. Mary and Michael both had dark chestnut hair and huge brown eyes. As Leslie jumped into the car, Mary smiled and waved at me, "Hello, Michelle long time no see." I explained to Leslie that her mom was my substitute teacher for math earlier in the school year. As they drove off, I walked the opposite direction towards home arguing with myself about how to proceed through this turn of events. It was an animated conversation!

I called my girlfriend as soon as I got home to tell her about meeting Leslie and how I couldn't allow myself to be her friend if I liked her brother. She agreed! Otherwise, it would appear like I used his sister to get closer to him. Her advice was to keep my friendship with Leslie limited to soccer practice only.

I was disheartened to be forced to chose. In one hand, I had my friendship with Leslie on the other, liking Michael.

Hopefully, Leslie will forgive me for my decision. I quit the soccer team.

Not all friends are peers.

Chapter 2

I was known as the school's peace maker. One day, Michael's girlfriend approached me. Apparently, he had broken up with her and was refusing to tell her why. I tried to explain to her that using me to mediate between them was a bad idea, but she insisted. She gave me his phone number and asked me to talk some sense back into him. I relented and, as requested, I called Michael on her behalf.

My inner teenage voice rejoiced to have an excuse to talk to him, but I had to remain calm. I wasn't allowed to call boys. But, since I wasn't calling for myself, I justified it as permissible. When I called to speak with Michael, he said he was heading to the pool; if I wanted, I could talk to him there. So, I went.

When I arrived at the pool, Michael was finishing his laps. My teenage heart had to be quieted as it attempted to beat out my chest. He wasn't only beautiful, but he was such a nice guy and super smart.

He loved to read science fiction books — me too! He was a movie buff — me too! He loved music — me too!

I kept my distance for three reasons: 1) His father was an officer, my father was enlisted, 2) He had an almost ex-girlfriend, and 3) I believed if you liked a boy and swam near him, you would get pregnant.

I wasn't taking any chances. I didn't dare put a toe in the water.

That night, I called his ex-girlfriend to give her my report. I explained to her that Michael simply didn't like her attitude when she didn't get her way. I let her know that he believed he had been patient with her for the months they dated and he simply didn't have much in common with her. She asked me to call him again and ask more questions. Back and forth I went between them for another week. Then, months passed without a word from his ex. She began dating someone new. Michael began inviting me to hang out with his group of friends. When Track and Field season began, we saw each other everyday after school. One day, his ex saw me at the gym and picked a fight with me about... guess what, HIM! She said I "stole him away."

It wasn't much of a fight. I simply refused to engage.

The next day at school, everyone was talking about the fight over Michael. He came to me.

"You fought for me?" he asked.

"No, I stopped her from screaming at me."

"You fought for me," he said again with his amazing smile.

That sealed the deal. We started officially dating and became the best of friends. He called me every night and would slip notes into my locker for me to find between classes. Michael made me laugh and I had never been more comfortable with anyone as I was with him. He started bringing me to Bible study with him on Friday evenings. I remember I enjoyed going, but the day he suggested he would pick me up on his Passport instead of the car, I freaked out a little. Sitting that close on the seat may be as dangerous as swimming! My girlfriend assured me that I had to do much more than sit close to get pregnant. I trusted her, but went to the encyclopedia to research pregnancy. I distinctly remember thinking, "Yuck! There is no way THAT is ever going to happen".

Soon after, Michael asked me to the Junior/Senior Prom. When the big dance arrived, I wore a white dress with a blue ribbon around my waist. He wore a dark blue suit. When we arrived at prom, our friends complimented us as a couple and said we looked like the topper of a wedding cake. Secretly, this made me very happy.

Our post-prom breakfast was hosted at the Mras house for all the friends of their three children, Jessica (senior), Michael (junior) and Leslie (freshman), to ensure we ate before we left on an hour-long bus trip to Subic Bay Naval Station. Mary greeted each of us with a big smile and was a gracious hostess. She brought quiche to the table. I had never had that type of dish before and it was delicious!

Michael, however, crinkled his nose at it.

"Real men don't eat quiche!" he exclaimed.

Mrs. Mras replied, "Then real men will be hungry, won't they?"

Her answer to Michael's comment was refreshing to me. I would have never thought of refusing food that my mother had graciously made for me and my friends. But, her calm, witty response was blunt, without demeaning or embarrassing to her son. They even smiled at each other as they exchanged words. She wasn't angry and he wasn't being disrespectful. They spoke as two people with opinions, not as a parent giving a direct order. This was unheard of in my world and I liked it. They were teasing each other back and forth with witty comebacks and jokes.

We arrived at Subic Bay in time to catch our 2-hour cruise to our beach party. During the cruise, I became more fascinated by Michael and his relationship with his family. I asked questions about how he was still alive after talking to his mother like an equal, and he informed me that his parents encouraged talking things out. They talked about everything. I was positive his family was just acting because no family can really be like the *Leave It to Beaver* television show. Michael was convinced that his parents trusted his decisions. I was in awe with the relationship he had with his parents, especially Mary.

> *You can't choose family. - Mary*
> *But, you can choose who you associate with. -*
> *Michael*

Michael's family was my fantasy version of family life. I was raised Philippine style where there is a hierarchy within the family. There is no-crossing line between younger and older siblings. Respect up the chain would never bend. The younger family members did what they were told and there was no arguing.

"This is my house. My rules!" my father often yelled.

Michael's family ran on a subject foreign to me — mutual respect and shared opinions.

Michael, the only son, once told me a story that distilled the essence of his relationship with Mary.

He was walking through the house toward the front door while Mary was hosting a group of her lady friends.

As he reached the door, Mary yelled out to him, "Remember what I always say!"

"No drinking. No bar girls"? Michael said without hesitation.

"No. The other thing" she said through her teeth.

"No one likes a smart ass?" Michael replied and ran out the door.

As the door shut, he heard his mother and the room of ladies laughing hysterically.

Sarcasm is a great second language.

Two short months later, my father was given orders to relocate to Offutt Air Force Base in Omaha, Nebraska. We would pack up the house and leave the Philippines forever within the next 30 days. Michael and his family were visiting the United States for the summer. This meant that I would be gone before he returned to the Philippines. You must remember that this happened before cell phones and the internet — Michael was essentially out of reach! Basically, our quick goodbye before he left was the last I would ever see of him. I told his best friend, Matt, that my family was PCS-ing (Permanent Change of Station) and to please kiss Michael goodbye for me.

I cried myself to sleep every night knowing I would never see Michael again. My family packed our luggage, the movers packed the house and we relocated into the temporary lodging quarters (TLQ) for our last two weeks in the Philippines. The last night of our stay, there was a knock at the door. I opened it to find Michael with his full Cheshire Cat smile, bearing a farewell Grasshopper ice cream pie from the new Baskin-Robbins. Michael informed me that Matt had told him I was leaving the country before his return. Michael immediately asked his parents if he could return to the Philippines early so that he could say goodbye. Michael had taken a 12-hour flight from Colorado to the Philippines to see me. I began to believe that he may actually really like me.

Actions speak louder than words.

Three hours later, when I walked Michael to the door, he hugged me tightly and lightly kissed me. Then, he slipped a small box into my hand. He insisted that I didn't open it until after he had left and he promised to come to the airport in the morning to say goodbye. He hugged me again, then quickly ran off. As he turned the corner, I opened the box. Inside was a single carat cubic zirconia on a chain. His affection was too good to be true, but I would never see him again. Once again, I cried myself to a very restless sleep.

The next day at the airport, while waiting to board our plane to the United States, I watched the door for Michael, but he didn't show. My parents had let me stay outside the secured area to wait for him. It was close to the time to board the Jumbo Jet, so I dejectedly went through the security check. I went to where my family was gathering up our bags. Filled with grief, I leaned against the glass partition.

Boom. Boom. Boom.

The glass to my back was being pounded upon. Michael had arrived to say goodbye. He didn't lie.

I asked to leave the restricted area, but wasn't allowed.

He was only inches away from me, but the glass was too thick for us to talk through.

Just like a movie, Michael and I stood silently, our hands placed palm to palm against the cool glass panel that separated us. It seemed as though time had stopped.

Then, Michael smiled and said what I believe was, "Olive Juice" and smiled.

I had no idea why he would say, "Olive Juice". I smiled back at him until my mother called me to walk out to the plane. I turned with tears in my eyes and waved goodbye.

Omaha? What's in Omaha?

Chapter *3*

Reality is all in the perspective.

Back in Omaha, school registration began and it was required to get a physical. I went to the base hospital, and to my surprise I saw a girl I knew from middle school at Clark AB. I was so excited to see a familiar face! Waving excitedly, I ran towards her. I was within 10 feet from her when she looked in my direction. Without a response, she looked back down and kept walking. She didn't even acknowledge my presence. Once again, I felt alone in a foreign world. The one day of the week I looked forward to was my call from Michael. Mrs. Mras would always say, "Hello" and ask how I was doing and provide little bits of encouragement until Michael could work the phone away from her. Those calls helped me though a rough transition period for me. Reaching out to familiar friends was comforting in a new place.

Good friends are the ones who are there when no one else wants to be bothered.

High school began and the time zone difference made it very hard to connect with Michael — he would be up when I was sleeping or vice versa. Michael's best friend, Matt began calling me on a monthly basis to remind me that Michael and I belonged together and that I should be careful not to break his heart. I made the promise even though I didn't understand what it meant. Two years passed. I received flowers and cards from Michael, but absence didn't make my heart grow fonder. My heart grew forgetful of how compatible we were together.

Even a rose has thorns.

Chapter *4*

Somewhere in the chaos of high school, the long distance relationship became too much. We mutually agreed to see other people. Despite that, we remained friends. I began my studies at the University of Nebraska as Michael began his second year at Texas A+M, Galveston, Texas. During this time, I received a photo of Michael and he had grown his hair long, shaved the sides of his head and looked much like a member of the band A Flock of Seagulls. He had begun wearing a lot of black, pierced his ear and to my conservative eyes, looked rather alarming. On our next call together, I asked him what Mary thought of his altered look.

He said, "My clothes don't change who I am. I'm still the same guy".

He continued to tell me the story he shared with Mary. People at his school were under the impression that he was a pothead because he hung out with the group known for drug use. He promised that he never touched drugs but, he really enjoyed their company and they listened to fantastic music.

After he told Mary the story, she said, "People have every right to dress and look the way they want. But, others have the right to treat them differently based upon their choice."

I told him, I understood and accepted his new look, but that I preferred more clean cut men.

In June 1990, Michael called to inform me that he had joined the US Air Force. He had graduated from college, accepted a commission and was moving to Tyndall Air Force Base, Panama City, Florida for training. During his training, he would call me every available chance he had. I would do my best to cheer him up from his stressful training. We made plans to one day see each other again. In March 1991, Michael finished training, and was assigned to McChord Air Force Base, Tacoma, Washington. Michael was driving there and made plans to visit me in Omaha on his way through. He met my friends including one man I thought I was resigned to one day marry. The two men did not get along well at all. My being in a new relationship clouded the fact that Michael still cared for me.

Once again, life went on. In November of 1991, Michael called with his credit card number and told me to purchase a ticket to visit him in Tacoma, Washington because he needed help decorating his apartment. My budget was tight and the loss of much needed wages made me hesitant to leave, but I found a week to visit him. Together, we chose his new furniture, dishes and silverware for his new apartment; we had a blast. During the visit we talked to his parents about all the fun tourist activities we were doing together after all these years apart. Mary loved that we were randomly exploring the area and discovering hole-in-the-wall shops and obscure restaurants.

> *Get lost on purpose. Find new routes to common places.*
> *Mary loved to get lost. She believed the experience opened a person for new experiences.*

In October 1992, Michael had just returned from 90 days in Saudi Arabia supporting the war in Iraq. Even there, he found a way to call me every week. As he described it, there was a commercial phone on the desk at work that no one knew where the bill went, and the only person he wanted to talk to was me. I was on my weekly call with Michael. It was late at night, and we got on the discussion of me thinking the man I was currently dating was about to propose. I respected Michael's opinion not only because I considered him my best friend and I wanted him to be my Man of Honor. If he didn't want to be my Man of Honor, I didn't know who I would want by my side. Although I couldn't see him, the tone of his voice became obviously agitated.

"Man of Honor? The man you marry should be your best friend."

"Don't be silly, Michael." I laughed, "You're my best friend. I would never compromise our friendship by marrying you."

He was dumb-founded by my response. He then went into a prolonged explanation of why I should consider marrying my best friend. With each point, I countered with my logic.

After several hours of debating he blurted out, "Marry me, Michelle. I'm the one you should marry!"

Silence filled the phone line.

"Did you just ask me to marry you?"

"Yes, I did," he replied calmly.

"Then, yes, I would gladly marry my best friend. I'd be honored to spend my life with you!"

Little did we know, but we had repeated how his parents started. Michael was the quiet thinker. I was the out-going extrovert. Michael knew we belonged together, and although when we met I believed we did too, I dismissed my teenage feelings as puppy love. It took Michael only hours to convince me that he truly was (and continues to be) my soul mate. I have never been happier to be wrong.

We talked late into the night. We made plans for when I would sell my furniture, end my apartment lease and finding a job before I arrived in Tacoma, Washington to be with him. The next morning I hesitantly went to see my boyfriend to let him know that I had accepted Michael's marriage proposal. I walked into the store where he worked: immediately, he knew something was very different.

"Michael asked you to marry him", he stated, not even asking it as a question.

"How did you know?"

"I just did. You were meant for each other. I'm happy for you," he replied with a disappointed, yet pleasant smile.

If you love someone, set them free.
If they don't come back, it wasn't meant to be.

When I returned to my apartment that evening, my phone rang. When I answered the line, there was an unfamiliar male voice on the other end.

"Welcome to the family," said a voice quite reminiscent of an airline pilot, "you can call me, Dad, if you'd like".

Then, a cheerful (and more familiar) female voice came over the phone line.

"It's about time! You two could have bought an island with all the money spent on phone calls for the past 9 years!"

"Mrs. Mras?" I was still trying to put this unexpected call into perspective.

"That will be your name soon enough. Call me, Mom! I'm so excited for the two of you. I always hoped he'd figure out the two of you belonged together."

Ah! That strange male voice who told me to call him Dad — that must have been Tony, Michael's father. Although I had met and spoken to Mary on several occasions, I had never spoken to him.

"Michelle, this is dad. Michael said you are an Engineering student."

"Yes, sir, I was. I just switched Majors." I responded fearful that he would be disappointed that his son was engaged to someone who gave up on a potentially lucrative career path.

"What caused you to switch degree programs?" He asked.

"I made it to Differential Equations and decided that I didn't want to do this for the rest of my life." I responded sheepishly.

"Me, too! I learned quickly in Diffy Qs that I was not meant for this career field." He laughed out as we discovered an instant empathetic bond.

Our conversation went on a while longer and we discovered we were both from the same sized family and both born in New Jersey. I'm sure Mary instigated this whole interaction. I learned that Mary had a talk with Michael weeks earlier about the importance of marrying your best friend. Michael's explanation to erase my reservations about marrying him was actually Mary's wisdom.

> *Don't look to get married. Marriage should not be your first goal.*
> *Seek to be financial stable and able to care for yourself.*
> *Then, when you meet someone, you don't "need" each other for support.*
> *You choose to be together. If it's meant to be, it will happen.*
> *If not, you'll learn what qualities you desire in your next prospect.*

August 1993 arrived. Ten years had passed since I first laid eyes on the awkward, gangly, beautiful 16-year-old boy back in the Philippines. Never in my wildest dreams had I pictured myself walking toward him on this beautiful, stormy day to the tune of Pachebel's Canon in D. Lightning flashed and shot colorful beams of light through the stained glass windows of the chapel. Boom. Boom. Boom. The thunder shook the chapel walls. Each "Boom" seemed to meld perfectly with the music as I walked toward my destiny.

With each step closer to Michael, I saw the smiling faces of family and friends who have known us as children and separately as young adults. Each face bringing flashes of memories. I saw Leslie's smile and knew she was happy I had to choose her brother over our friendship. Then, I saw Mary's smile and my smile back increased as I reflected on her words to Michael and I during the reception dinner the night prior.

"Michelle, promise me you'll give Michael a vice!" Mary insisted, "He's too methodical and logical. Make him loosen up a little."

"She is my vice." Michael replied calmly with a smirk upon his face.

My father and I reached the altar. I looked at this stunningly handsome man before me and he mouthed, "Olive Juice" and smiled.

My father passed my hand to Michael, and as he did, the storm stopped and the sun light burst in an array of rainbow colors throughout the chapel.

My father leaned down to kiss my cheek and whispered, "He's a good man".

"I know." I smiled back, "He saved the best for last".

Good things come to those that wait.

10-years in the making, marrying Michael was the best day and the best decision of my life. I found a life-long friend who loved me and just happened to belong to a family who openly took me in as one of their own.

Chapter 5

It was November 1993 when we had our first visit as a married couple to my in-laws' home in Fairfield, California. Michael and I were living in Tacoma, Washington and had driven down for a visit. Tony broke out the red wine and Mary set out some goblets and we began a deep discussion that lasted late into the night about our life plans as a newlywed couple.

> *Your relationship with your spouse is the foundation of the family; It takes priority above all. Whenever any of the children complained one child was being favored over another, Mary would simply say with a gentle smile, "That's because I like them best".*

Our plan for every aspect of our lives together was up for discussion: career paths, college, savings, Individual Retirement Accounts, children, adoption, spending plans, credit cards, vacationing, language we will use when we are upset, etc. Michael and I had a lot of thinking to do.

Wait on children: Get to know each other, first. Dating and marriage aren't always the same. One day your children will move out. You need to know you still have similar interests. Have date nights throughout your marriage.

Mary and Tony advised us to talk about everything that may come up in our lives before they occurred. Discussing possible situations before they arose gave us a plan of how we'd approach a potential problem before we were in the middle of it. We were advised that the best way to avoid knee-jerk reactions was to have a plan, however tentative. It was going to be a lot of work, but if we wanted to emulate a relationship as successful as Mary and Tony's marriage, we needed to follow suit.

We needed to have a plan.

Every decision needs a well thought plan.

The next morning we were awakened by loud Broadway music coming from the living room — little did I know that this would become a morning tradition for all our visits. Mary was singing at the top of her lungs to Little Shop of Horrors as she did her culinary magic in the kitchen. I followed my nose down the stairs, guided by the smell of rich roasted, freshly brewed coffee. As I reached the main floor, I joined Mary's one-woman show by singing along with the music at the top of my lungs. I was turning the corner to reach the kitchen, when Michael ran past me, slid into the kitchen and exclaimed,

"Mom is great! She got us chocolate cake!"

Sure enough, when I entered the kitchen, there was a chocolate cake and a strawberry pie sitting on the kitchen table. That was it. No breakfast items at all, which explains why I didn't smell bacon and eggs.

Mary was leaning against the kitchen island with her coffee cup held close to her nose and she had a pleasant smile on her face as she enjoyed the simple pleasure of the smell of her coffee. Tony sat quietly at the table enduring the now two-woman Broadway show and reading the morning paper as he waited for breakfast. The four of us gathered at the table around the breakfast of desserts and coffee to continue our talk from the night before. Before we actually continued the discussion, Mary felt compelled to explain why we were having dessert for breakfast. Her reasoning was simple.

"I want to enjoy your company, if I was cooking breakfast I wouldn't be engaged in the conversation. So, Tony and I went out and purchased our favorites from the bakery down the street."

There will be differences of opinion; choose your battles.

If one feels strongly about a subject, the other can concede and vice-versa.

Her logic made perfect sense. Mary knew that we needed to enjoy dessert first and savor the quality time we rarely had the opportunity to have. Her subtle message was that dessert was not just this one moment in time, but in all the little moments in our lives. Her message was to take the time to smell the flowers, to laugh, to sing, to dance, to hold hands and most important, to do what brings us happiness.

Life is short, we need to eat dessert first.

Later that day, we decided to eat out for supper. After settling at our table, we discussed what each of us were ordering.

Michael announced.

"I always get this dish, it's delicious".

Tony smiled because he knew what was coming.

Mary said, "Rut and a grave. Try something else."

I was perplexed. Michael explained that his mom was a big proponent of the saying, "The differences between ruts and graves are the dimensions". Based on the look on my face, Mary surmised that I had no idea how her logic applied to food.

She then explained her concept more fully in that people are creatures of habit. If left to their own instinct and without intentional actions, people naturally fall into ruts where they get stuck. Then, one day, they look up and realize that they have never accomplished their dreams because they were so focused in staying in their routine.

As humans, we wake up, go to work, come home, eat dinner, go to sleep, and wake up just to repeat the cycle. We unconsciously build the dimensions to our ruts.

If we aren't living our lives to the fullest, then we are already dead – we have simply exchanged our rut for our grave. We just don't realize it.

Mary encouraged the mentality: if you always do the same thing, stop! Get out of your rut before it becomes your grave.

Avoid ruts.

When our food arrived, Mary suggested we share bites of our food with each other. In my mind, it was like a scene from the Mad Hatter's table in Lewis Carrol's Alice's Adventures in Wonderland.

"Switch plates! Switch plates! Move down!" — insanity mixed with adventure.

This was just a taste of life with Mary. We never knew exactly what she would do. Her lesson? Keep people guessing. Better yet, keep yourself on edge by forcing yourself out of comfort zones.

Mary's curiosity and sense of adventure took her to try new things her entire life. She excelled at horseback riding as a child and skiing as a teen. Throughout her marriage with Tony, she was forever reaching out to learn to play the guitar, excel at yoga, sing in a choir, understand globalization, whatever. Many of these were not sustained, but she felt strongly that you needed to try something to see if it was a for you. She was not one to follow the herd; she trusted her own judgement and experiences.

> *The only difference between a rut and a grave are the dimensions.*
>
> *— Ellen Glasgow*

As the newest Mrs. Mras, I learned a lot that first visit. Each subsequent visit was enjoyable and enlightening in many ways. The culture surrounding my new family was different from the family dynamic in which I had been raised. I loved every moment! As a new couple trying to find our way, Michael and I spoke with Mary and Tony many times per week for hours at a time. It wasn't a chore; rather, it was a sincere pleasure to discuss our lives with our marriage mentors.

October 1993, Michael and I made our first large purchase as a married couple, a blue Mazda Miata 2-

door convertible. We had gone to the dealer with a practical car purchase in mind, but we passed the cute little sports car on the lot.

I remarked, "Michael, we should get this. We could drive a fun car while we're young instead of waiting until we're older."

When we called the in-laws to tell them the news, Mary was overjoyed.

"Oh how fun and irresponsible! Good job, Michelle!"

Chapter *6*

The US Air Force was preparing to send Michael to South Korea for a one-year remote assignment. Actually, he volunteered for the assignment since we decided he would be required to do a remote assignment during his career, he might as well do it while we are young and without children. We knew our relationship could survive a year apart, we had certainly done it before. Before the remote assignment, Michael was sent to a survival school in Spokane, Washington. Since I was alone in Tacoma, Mary and Tony invited me down to visit them. Visiting them was always a treat. I loved the deep discussions we'd get into and the two-women Broadway shows we would perform together; Mary loved to play the piano and I never pass an opportunity to sing.

One evening, as Mary and I began to prepare dinner, she pulled out an 8-ounce ribeye steak and some spinach. Tony took the steak to grill it in the backyard while Mary was busy chopping veggies for the salad. She asked me to assemble the salad, advising me that the salad dressing was one that she made in a small Pyrex bowl placed in the refrigerator. I looked around the fridge without luck.

"I can't find the dressing, is there another place it could be?" I asked.

"Second shelf on the door, just under the butter." Mary replied.

"I only see a small bowl of bacon grease." I responded.

"That's it. It's not bacon grease. Just heat it up a little and drizzle it over the salad greens." she sang with her up beat attitude.

"I made Italian dressing two nights ago. It just solidified. Trust me." She said.

Mary prided herself on the ability to make a meal out of anything in the refrigerator. When she and Tony were newlyweds, Mary created a casserole out of sardines, cheese and potatoes.
Why? Because she could.

Tony came back in with the cooked steak and Mary began to cut the tiny steak into three equal pieces. I had done as requested and poured the "dressing" onto the salad greens and tossed it along with the other veggies she had sliced. The three of us sat at the table, each with a glass of red wine, a healthy serving of salad and roughly a 2-ounce steak. Tony had heard the discussion about the bacon grease and had started eating the meat. Mary began with the salad. I watched, drinking my wine. Tony was done with his steak in two bites.

Mary placed her second fork-full of salad into her mouth and looked slightly amused.

"You know what?" she said between bites, "I think that really is bacon grease. It's not that horrible."

Tony and I did not eat the salad.

After dinner, we sat and had a cup of coffee. Tony looked at me and said with his calm voice that comes so naturally to pilots,

"Michelle, would you accompany me on my walk with the dog?"

"No thank you, Dad. I don't want to interrupt your alone time," I responded.

"I want you to come with me." Tony said in a voice that sounded like I had no choice.

This was rather strange of him, since Tony rarely spoke and even more rarely with such insistence.

Tony, Ebony (the dog) and I went for our walk. Interestingly, Tony turned and went in the opposite direction from his normal path. I didn't question him. We walked in silence with Tony only occasionally speaking to the dog. We turned away from the direction of the neighborhood and instead headed down the main street toward the highway.

"Dad, where are we going?" I was becoming concerned.

I never called him, Tony.

"You'll see." was his mysterious reply.

Three <u>miles</u> of silence later, we arrived at a Wendy's fast food restaurant. Tony looked at me, smiled and said, "I'm starving! I need meat. I've added this stop to my nightly walk so I don't wither away. I love Mary, but her meat portions are tiny ever since the doctor suggested we reduce our red meat consumption."

Love is… walking six miles round trip to find food.

My relationship with Tony changed that evening. We laughed about the 8-ounce steak being cut to serve three people. We each ate our fries and bacon cheeseburgers while sitting on the curb outside of Wendy's. We giggled with amusement that Mary was so stubborn — she would eat bacon grease rather than admit she was wrong! As we got up to return home, Tony handed me a piece of gum.

"This should help mask the smell of meat on us."

We walked the three miles back home in complete silence, with smiles on our faces. We bonded that night. It was fabulous.

Before Michael's departure to South Korea, we visited Tony and Mary. On this trip, Michael and I arrived and Mary said that she had discovered the best thing since sliced bread — Cardboardeux. She drank alcohol, but Tony would only enjoy an occasional glass. This frustrated her because she did not want to allow a bottle of wine to go to waste. The discovery of boxed wine solved her dilemma.

"Michelle, come finish this box of wine with me. There really are only two glasses left. Tony, please pick up another box of wine for us." Mary directed.

Mary trusted her judgement. Where others bought the expensive wines from exotic wineries, she believed that wine was as good as the company you share it with. Regardless of what the critics of box wines said, Mary believed the lesson was that appearances and trappings were not as important as our own judgement.

Boxed wine is good wine.

I wasn't much of a wine drinker, but it was only one glass, and it was with Mary. She poured two glasses from the box.

She shook the box and said, "We might be able to get another half a glass each out of what's left."

Four glasses later, Mary and I were laughing about everything, especially how deceptive the level of wine can be in a box. There's a lot more in them than it appears.

The men came home to find us crying with laughter as we were drinking from the now removed plastic bag that held the wine in the box. We had removed the bag and had cut a small hole in one of the corners to save the last drops of wine from being cast away. They wouldn't open another box for us that night.

Chapter 7

Families, if at all possible, should stay together.

Two weeks later, Michael left for his one-year remote assignment to Osan Air Base in Osan, South Korea. This meant that I wasn't permitted to move with him. Although I was disappointed, I understood the commitment required to be a military spouse. Holding true to Mary's advice, I ended up visiting twice for 90 days at a time. Before I left for my first visit to South Korea, I spent time with Mary and Tony. Mary became fixated on a silverware service that was supposedly made in South Korea. She specifically asked me to find her a set and let her know the price so she could have me purchase it for her direct from the factory. I agreed, and when I arrived in South Korea in May 1995, I began touring the markets of Seoul and the surrounding areas. I was on a quest to find silverware.

South Korea may look small on a map, but there are a lot of people that leads to congestion within the cities and shopping centers. Michael accompanied me and assisted me in my quest. After walking through an enormous market in northern Seoul without success, our next trip was to the shopping market in southern Seoul. No luck. There were silverware sets, but not a Western traditional set. These consisted of a large spoon and a pair of thin metal chopsticks.

When I reported back to Mary that what she sought didn't exist, she said, "No worries, when Tony and I visit, we'll look, too". When they arrived several months after I left, they looked and had no better luck than I did.

"Mom, I don't think the company is in South Korea. If it is, perhaps they only export them. People in South Korea don't use forks," explained Michael.

Mary and Tony explored all the markets I explored during their visit. The enormity of the markets dampened Mary's quest to find the silverware sets. If they were for sale, they were not common.

Chapter 8

When Michael's remote was over, he was offered a job flying with the North Atlantic Treaty Organization (NATO). This assignment was too awesome to pass up. We would live in a German village and raise our soon to arrive first child in Europe. We were so excited! We called Mary and Tony to share the exciting news and Mary immediately began making plans to visit us in the land of beer and wine.

"Just think of all the beer and wine you'll have the privilege of trying!" Mary exclaimed.

When Michael reminded her he didn't drink alcohol, we could hear the disappointment in her voice that all the sampling would go to waste. She tried to explain to Michael that he wouldn't get the full experience of Europe if he didn't at least try.

When Michael responded with, "Should I turn down the assignment?"

She said mockingly said, "Yes"!

We reminded her that I, Michelle, drank alcohol and would gladly taste test with her across Europe.

Mary vowed to come visit and remedy Michael's failure to taste test European alcohol. Mary wasn't a heavy drinker, she simply didn't need alcohol to enjoy life. But, to be in Europe and sample alcohol from the source was an adventure she could not pass up.

Don't pack more than you can carry. This is an analogy for life.
As a military family, the family purged excess from their home with each move.
Bring with you only the things you need for the next
leg of your journey.

The move to Geilenkirchen NATO Air Base, Germany arrived. Our sponsor to the foreign land found us a nice townhouse to temporarily call home while we searched for a house to rent on the local economy. Our phone calls back to the United States were frequent. At the end of each week we called Mary and Tony sharing our adventures or to explain the travel photos we had sent home. Mary would mark on her map all the places we visited and she took note of places she definitely wanted to visit.

Make it a priority to have alone time with your children individually.

Do the same with your grandchildren.

A few months later we welcomed 1997 and our first child. As promised, Mary and Tony came to Europe and Mary did her civic duty of rescuing all the lonely beers and wines from her son's neglect. Mary insisted she and Tony have alone time with their newest grandbaby to provide Michael and I much needed sleep and down time. Early in their visit, I woke abruptly after I realized our three-month-old didn't wake me. I had slept in. Michael and I went downstairs following the obvious up to no good sounds.

We could hear laughter and giggles from Mary and Tony. Mary was making airplane flying sounds as we rounded the corner to the kitchen.

"Open big for Grandma," we heard Mary saying in her melodic voice.

As we entered the kitchen, we discovered Tony holding a very happy baby with her hands reaching for a small spoon held by Mary. They looked at us and simultaneously burst out with guilty laughter. They were giving our baby taste samples of every condiment in the refrigerator and she was enjoying every minute of it.

"What are you doing? She's not on solid foods." Michael interrupted.

"She is now! We're just giving her tiny samples of all the wonderful tastes in the world and she loves it!" The giddy grandparents were having a ball. Between tastes, they were feeding our daughter Grandpa's oatmeal.

Give children choices.
Mary had a rule when her children were young, that each could choose their own cereal with the caveat that the first ingredient wasn't sugar. Then, she'd keep the toys from the cereal box until she had enough to distribute them evenly among the three children.

Mary had a knack with maps. Whenever we travelled, she would ask us where we were and track our travel and estimate the times we would arrive at our next destination. Being in Germany intensified her desire to play navigator for all our road trips throughout Europe. Mary took pride in providing directions during their visit. It didn't raise any concerns for her that she didn't speak or read German or Flemish. As long as she knew which direction we were headed, she was confident she would be the perfect guide.

There was an unaddressed problem with her internal guidance system. She grew up in Eastern Colorado, and whenever she saw a mountain range she instinctively thought of it as west. To add a twist to the normal north, south, east, west directions, German roads are not labeled with compass coordinates. Cities are identified by the next city. You need to know which city is next and in what direction in order to navigate properly. Michael had to consistently remind her which direction we were traveling if the sun was directly overhead.

One of our first ventures out with Mary as our navigator, we headed to the city of Aachen, Germany. We were well on our way, when Mary seemed confused.

"I know we're here [pointing at the map] and we're going here [pointing at Aachen on the map]. All the highway signs are pointing to a city I don't see on the map."

"What city?" Michael asked.

"The city must be huge! All the signs we've passed indicate, ASFARHT. Where the hell is Asfarht, Germany?"

"Mom," Michael and I began to laugh, "ASFARHT means EXIT in German".

"Well, that makes things clearer," she said with a smirk on her face.

To assume makes an Ass of U and Me.

We travelled all around Germany showing my in-laws the sights, castles, cathedrals, wineries and daily life in the tri-country area of Germany, Netherlands and Belgium. One of our trips was to Heidelberg, Germany to see the huge castle at the top of the mountain. There we stayed at a lovely bed and breakfast. Mary made tour plans for the city. After breakfast of dark, rich coffee and an assortment of cold cuts, breads, jams and cheeses, we headed out to venture through the historic and gorgeous city.

Mary's plan started us at Philosopher's Way. According to the tour map, it promised to be a beautiful trail that would bring the visitor to views of the whole countryside. When we arrived at the base of the mountain, the path seemed to disappear around a corner at a steep 45-degree angle. No big deal, we have a stroller, this angle is probably just at the start. Plus, Mary assured us the brochure described it as a stunningly beautiful and leisurely stroll. The path's incline did not dissipate; rather, it continued at the 45-degree angle with an occasional respite of a 15-degree angle. At each turn, Mary would give out encouraging words about the particular location being the last of the hard spots and the path would level out soon. Two hours into our walk, Mary stopped in her tracks.

"The brochure lied!" She said out of breath, "Well, we've come so far we might as well keep going. At least we know down hill will be super easy!"

After another mile or so, Mary started us in a fit of giggles.

"Germans apparently have a different idea of what should be considered leisurely!" she declared.

"Germans?" Michael laughed, "Your maiden name is Kohlrieser!"

Our sore calves screamed louder than our exhausting hysteria as we continued our ascent.

We finally reached the majestic top and the view was truly spectacular. As a huge bonus for Mary and I, there was a winery at the top! We relaxed our calves and recovered a long while before we headed back down.

Mary had an epiphany.

"I know why they call it Philosopher's Way. The scholars would walk up this intensely painful hill all the while philosophizing the insanity of walking up it".

Enjoy the journey. It is just as important as your destination.

With Mary's unique German map reading skills, we managed to get lost and found in multiple countries. This, however, never diminished Mary's desire to be in control of the map. Another trip brought us through a vibrant German city during what was probably their rush hour. We drove into a huge ring around downtown. As we drove in circles, Mary kept saying, "No, that's not it".

Michael was tired of driving in circles, "Mom, what street are we looking for?"

"Don't worry, I've got this. I'll know it when I see it" replied Mary.

A few more loops around and Michael said, "Mom, let us help".

"The street is spelled, E-i-n-Ban-s-t-r-a-then a funny line with a 3 attached, and an e," she said exasperated.

This time, I replied, "Mom, that spells, Einbanstrasse."

"Yes, exactly." Mary replied.

"That means, one-way street." I explained.

"Well, that explains a lot. I guess we're here." Mary mumbled and then she laughed which made us all laugh with her.

If you can't laugh at yourself, you are way too serious.

One of Mary's goals while in Europe was to take a picture of the 'typical' German house. She explained that it would be a one level, white stucco home, with a thatched roof and vines of flowers cascading over the door arch; the typical German house in all the old movies. We took many side streets throughout Germany looking for this house.

Michael asked, "Mom, if the house is so typical, shouldn't we see that type of house at every turn?"

Mary would not be distracted. She was on a quest.

People give up right before they would have succeeded.
Never give up.

During the second week of the visit, Mary and Tony went alone to France to explore for a few days. This was a big treat since French was the language they spoke to each other when they didn't want us to know what they were saying.

The City of Love was a bucket list item for them. They feasted on baguettes, cheeses, sausages and wine for the several days of their visit. Mary was in Heaven.

When they returned to Germany, Tony told us quietly what had happened on their first day of touring Paris. Tony had read all of the travel books and planned the travel through Paris via the outstanding subway system. Mary was appalled that anyone would travel underground when there was so much to see above ground.

When the debate was over, Mary had won. They would travel above ground on a bus so they could see the sights. A big lesson was quickly learned. If you want to see Paris, travel underground. It had taken them almost an hour to travel a block! Tony said he could have walked faster than the bus had moved through the bumper-to-bumper traffic. Mary never admitted defeat, but they had taken the subway the rest of the trip. They then had taken advantage of all the extra time that the subway provided them, acting like lovebirds, sitting outside at local bistros and soaking in the culture that is uniquely Paris.

Once you get off the street, Paris is for lovers.

When Tony and Mary returned from Paris, there were two days left for Mary to get her photo of the 'typical' German house. We were out for a drive on the last afternoon when Mary screamed from the backseat.

"Stop! I told you it existed"!

She jumped out of the car with her camera raised to finally capture the photo she had so desperately sought out; the 'typical' German house. She crossed to the other side of the street and began taking multiple photos. It was a stunning home. Just as she envisioned, it was a ranch style, white stucco home with evergreen colored shutters. The door was an old dark wood with black cast iron hinges. There was an arch of small pink roses and ivy on a trellis before the door. The thatched roof had thick moss growing on it making it appear as if the home was a cupcake frosted with a vibrant green icing. The whole house was tucked between a grove of tall lush evergreen trees. It was like a fairy-tale house and Mary beamed with delight as she continued to take pictures.

Tony said, "Finally, the trip is complete. She can mark this off her bucket list."

Michael looked at his dad and said, "We're in the Netherlands."

Tony replied, "Shhh, don't tell her, she's on a roll."

We all quietly smiled holding our secret when Mary returned to the car. She was so proud of herself to find the house depicted in all our fairy tale stories. Mary and Tony left Europe with great memories and left us with a new baby who, as a result of their actions, refused to eat bland baby food ever again.

Sometimes it's best to hold your tongue.

Chapter *9*

In the summer of 1998, we received a call from Mary that would change our world. She said circumstances had changed and the thought of coming to Europe for Christmas was no longer an option. She asked if we could come back to California instead. I told her it would be perfect timing for us to come back since our second child was due in September, and it would be wonderful for the whole family to meet the new baby and see how much our first child had grown.

We chatted for awhile and Mary spoke to her granddaughter who was now 15-months old. When she got back on the phone with me, I could tell there was something that she wanted to say, but that she was holding back.

"Mom, what's going on? Is Dad's health okay?"

I worried that Tony's prostate cancer had resurfaced. Three years prior to the European vacation, Tony had learned that he had prostate cancer. The family had flown back to be with them. There were several options available, but Mary was firm, "I want that cancer out." There were two possible probable after-effects of the surgery - incontinence or impotency. Mary's support allowed them to take their life changes in stride. Tony had had the operation and was cleared of his cancer, but it's never a good idea to relax when cancer is involved.

"Dad is fine considering the circumstances," Mary began, "do you want the good news or the bad news?"

Bracing for the worst, I hesitantly responded.

"I'll take the bad news". It will make the good news that much better.

Mary asked, "Remember that rowing machine I bought and rarely use?"

"Yes."

"Well, I've been losing weight and I thought I should be excited, but I haven't really worked out at all."

"Okay. Have you changed your eating habits?"

"No, not at all. I've done nothing to lose weight. I found a hard knot in my abdomen. So, I went to the doctor. They did a lot of blood work and the results have come back. We got a second opinion before we worried the family with speculation. There's no mistake. (Long pause) I have leukemia."

Silence filled the phone line.

I was filled with grief and anxiety. How could the woman I thought was the epitome of life be the one with a death sentence? Why? Dear God, please let this be a mistake. I cried out in my mind.

More silence.

Mary broke it with, "Do you want to hear the good news?"

I was thinking, the only good news I want to hear is that there is a cure and this is a sick joke.

My silence was too much.

Mary responded with, "I'm not dead, yet!"

The glass isn't half-full or half-empty; it's refillable.

Of course, she's right. Mary was more than a "glass half full" thinker. She knew all glasses were refillable. Laughing through my tears, I asked if she was in pain and how was dad handling this news? Did she want to tell Michael directly or did she want me to have him call her?

The toughest woman I know asked me to break the news to Michael gently and have him call her.

During our conversation, Mary informed me that she planned to fight this disease. But, before her treatment started, she wanted to spend Christmas of 1998 with her entire family. We made plans to return to the States immediately after our second child was born. We had to acquire a Certificate of Live Birth Abroad and then, apply for a US Passport to leave the country with our newborn. By the time I delivered our second child, completed all the legal paperwork and bought plane tickets to California, two and a half months had passed.

It was early December before we managed to arrive in California. Mary was encouraged to start her chemotherapy. As much as she wanted to hold off until after the holidays, it wasn't a good idea if she planned to beat leukemia; she was a fighter! She underwent her first series of chemotherapy leaving her immune system very weak. She was fortunate, however, to be given a bone marrow transplant from her older brother, John, who amazingly, was a perfect match.

The doctors were leery about her being around young children. It didn't matter to Mary. She was going to hold her grandbabies.

She insisted all her grandchildren come to the house. All three of her children made it home for the holidays: The two elder children with their spouses and children and the youngest daughter, Leslie, with her fiancé.

When we arrived at the house in California, the interior looked as if a professional decorator had been given free rein of the house. Small white Christmas lights adorned multiple wreaths and there were multiple

Christmas trees in the front window. We had entered a Christmas haven of peace, love and hope. This stunning visual reminder provide us all with the strength needed to help Mary and her battle with Cancer.

Michael and I were amazed at how well she handled the Chemo treatments. She ate what she wanted to include her favorite Butter Pecan ice cream. She drank her cardboardeux wine. Aside from her hair loss, Mary was the same woman full of energy and humor as she has always been.

How do you know if you don't try.

Having lost her hair as a result of her cancer treatments, Mary purchased a high-end wig that looked just like her normal hair. During our visit, our eldest child followed her Grandma everywhere. When it came time to sleep she wanted to stay with Grandma. She followed Mary to take a bath in Grandma's big tub. While in the bathroom, she saw a mannequin head that would later hold the wig.

"What's that, Grandma?" our 21 month old asked about the wig head.

"Oh, that's my other head" Mary responded.

"Grandma, you have two heads?" asked the toddler.

"Yes, I'm Grandma 2-Heads" Mary exclaimed with amusement.

The name stuck. Mary was forever renamed Grandma 2-Heads by our children.

Children are curious. Never punish them for asking questions.

While undergoing treatment, Mary decided that she needed an Airedale puppy. They named her Sassy. Sassy was everything Mary was not feeling - youthful, carefree and energetic with her long healthy life ahead of her.

Michael recalled the day during the early 1980s when his family went to a farm to pick out a family dog. The kids all fell in love with a cute, but not so bright, male puppy. Mary insisted on getting the shy female miniature Schnauzer puppy. When asked, "Why?" Mary explained that the female was brilliant and had personality. She explained when the family entered the area where the puppies were playing, all the other puppies ran out to greet the strangers. All except the female, Ramona. She sat away and watched the commotion. Ramona was an observer and therefore smarter. The family ended up getting the male puppy for Mary's mother. They named him Max, after Major Maxwell — an ode to the Major rank that Tony had received while stationed at Maxwell Air Force Base, Alabama

Choose a dog with a personality.

Chapter *10*

Mary played piano, sang, read and loved each of her four grandchildren. It was a beautiful visit. We cooked, sang and laughed a lot. Her youngest daughter's wedding was set for the following year, but they arranged for a small wedding ceremony to be held while the family was visiting, just in case Mary was too ill to attend the big ceremony. The family, as always, had a plan (as Mary had always taught us) but we all realized some plans were meant to be adjusted.

The two week family get-together was exactly what the doctor ordered to keep Mary's spirits up. It gave everyone a sense of hope to see Mary strong and determined as ever. The good times, however, were somewhat bittersweet. We had no guarantee that Mary would still be around for our next visit.

It was an emotional struggle when it came time to leave California. The night before we left, Mary had all her grandbabies around her on the couch as she read, Jon Stone and Michael Smollin's, *There's a Monster At*

The End Of This Book. Together they screamed and squealed in delight as Grandma brought the story to life with her assortment of voices and her ability to bring the suspense of the book, repeatedly, to her young audience.

Laughter is the best medicine.

Chapter *11*

For three years, Mary fought the leukemia battle. In and out of hospitals. In and out of treatment. Positive upswings in health followed by quick terrifying turns that tainted our prayerful hearts. Each experience was tasking for Mary and of course, Tony, who was always by her side. Through all the ups and downs, Mary was finally cleared of her leukemia, but her body had been ravished by the cancer and the chemotherapy in addition to all the illnesses this battle made her susceptible to catch.

During that time, we had moved back to the United States to Robins Air Force Base, Warner Robins, Georgia. It was May of 2001. Michael had just began training and needed special permission to travel. Our young daughters were in school, so Michael went back to visit Mary and Tony without us. He spent a week with his parents helping with handyman chores that had moved to the bottom of the list of priorities since Mary was ill. Michael cooked and spent much needed quality time with both parents. He was relieved to see his mother recovering from her long battle. When he returned to Georgia, he assured me that although Mary had a long road to a full recovery, she was doing well.

Our calls with Mary resumed from weekly back to nightly calls. Mary delighted in hearing of the adventures of the little Mras grandbabies as they grew into creative and brilliant children. Months passed and life began to resume normalcy. That was until we received a call from Mary's sister, Joyce, that all was not well. Mary wasn't as far out of the woods as we thought. After her visit to California, she thought the children should come home to visit. She alluded to the strength in Mary being the calm before the storm. It was a difficult decision, but as we weighed the decision to go back, the world was shaken.

September 11, 2001 — the world was shocked as America was attacked by terrorists. Michael's squadron was put on high alert and immediately began flying more frequently. We continued our daily calls with Mary and Tony to discuss the state of America.

The conversations felt odd, even when considering the subject matter. We couldn't place our finger on it, but his parents seemed detached.

After one of the calls, Michael turned to me and said, "That was the oddest conversation I have ever had with my mother."

"What do you mean?"

"I don't know. She seems not herself."

"Do you think you should go back to visit?"

"No, America's at war. I need to stay and do my duty."

Don't be afraid. They train well. They know what they're doing.

On September 17th, Michael received a call from Tony. Mary had developed a bruise that was traveling up her leg and had moved to her side. She was back in the hospital. Earlier that day, Mary was looking for something yummy to eat. She decided on Butter Pecan ice cream. When Tony arrived home, he found Mary sitting at the kitchen table enjoying her ice cream directly from the container. He asked about the pained look upon her face.

She explained, "The ice cream was on the top shelf of the freezer. So, I used a large spoon to knock it down. The frozen box hit my leg and now, my leg hurts."

Tony took a look at her leg and it was badly bruised, "I have to get you to the hospital."

"I'm tired of being poked on. I just need to rest," was Mary's request.

Tony did as requested of him, but checked on her again and noticed the bruise was traveling up her leg and had moved to her side. Despite Mary's judgement, she was back in the hospital.

Michael asked if he should come home, and Tony said, "Your mother will be okay, I'll call if anything changes."

His will be done.

The next day, Michael went to work as usual. Despite my urging for us to leave for California, he wanted to remain calm. I dropped the girls off at school and as I was driving to the store, I received a call from Tony.

He sounded scared.

"Michelle, you need to get here quickly. Mary has slipped into a coma. She has a living will to not revive her if she turns for the worse."

"We'll get there as soon as possible," I promised holding in my sobs of anguish. I didn't want Tony to comfort me. Like Mary, I had to be strong for him and Michael.

Being the spouse of a military member takes
bravery to a new level.
We need to be strong so they can do their jobs
without worrying about home.

I called Michael's squadron only to be told they were already in the air.

"Dear God!" I thought to myself. "His mother is passing away and he'll be in the air for at least six more hours."

I was connected to his Commander, Lieutenant Colonel Willie Nunn. I explained what was happening. I don't know what his Commander had to do, but he was determined to help get us to Mary's side.

"I'll get Michael back. We'll make flight arrangements for your family. Pack and be here to pick Michael up in two hours."

"Thank you," was all that I mustered to say.

Within the two hours I had packed for the family and was sitting in the Commander's office as we waited for Michael's plane to land. I explained to the Commander that Michael was the only son and that he was very close to his mother. I repeatedly thanked him for getting Michael back quickly and for making all the flight arrangements. I honestly don't know where I found the strength to remain calm.

The Commander met Michael on the flight line and brought him directly to his office. When Michael entered, the Commander had Michael sign papers authorizing him to go on leave and said, "Now, go catch your plane." As we headed off to pick up our children, poor Michael was in a daze as I explained that Tony had called and said we had to get home immediately. We picked up our youngest daughter from pre-school and were on our way to the elementary school when we received the call from Tony.

Mary was at peace.

As per her wishes, life support was unplugged.

I pulled over on the side of the road until I could gather my senses enough to drive safely. We held each other as we cried. Mary, the light of the family, was gone. Realizing the pain wasn't going to stop, I began to drive to pick up our eldest daughter. I don't remember the drive to the Atlanta airport, I just know we left for California a week after 9/11. There were only six passengers on the flight; the four of us and two other men.

We arrived in California and somehow managed to make it to the house. There were so many arrangements to be made for her funeral: food for the reception, choosing an urn for her ashes, writing 'Thank You' cards for all the sympathy cards and flowers. So much to do. Tony was a quiet mess. He was never a man of many words, but he was empty without Mary.

On September 24th, we said our public goodbye to a wonderful woman. People from throughout her life came to her service. There were former students, teachers, friends from their life in the military; people from all walks of life that came to celebrate her life.

Mary had touched so many lives simply by being the teacher, mentor, friend, principal, sister, mother and wife she was. She shared her smile and positive attitude with everyone she met.

As I watched those who joined us that day, I realized we weren't crying because she hadn't lived long enough. We cried because we no longer had the light which was Mary in our lives.

During the wake, many people had the opportunity to discuss how much Mary had meant to them. I loved hearing all of their stories, as I could see Mary's positive energy in everything that they were describing. I had been so focussed on all of my emotions and all of the people at the wake that I realized that I was somewhat hungry. Mindlessly, I went to the dessert table to get something to eat. Suddenly, I felt as if Mary was smiling down at me....

Updates on Mary From Tony

Tony and Mary met on a blind date at an Air Force
Academy cadet party during Tony's junior year.
The party organizer thought it would be funny to set up
two people with extremely different personalities.

Mary was an out-going, fun-loving, extrovert.
Tony was the quiet, stolid, plodder.

When they kissed in the coat closet,
Tony said he knew she was his soul mate.
It took him another year to convince her he was hers.

Wednesday, May 23, 2001 @ 12:23AM

Just a short update

Since Mary's return home on April 27, she has worked hard to stay independent and master the walker and wheelchair for mobility. Somewhere in the process, her eyesight has deteriorated to near nothing, her manual dexterity has dropped to minimal, her right foot has declared independence and does whatever it wants, her skin has become paper thin and is easily torn, and the pain in her butt (not me) has continued to challenge her. She attempted to e-mail a greeting to you all yesterday, but gave it up when she could neither see the monitor screen nor hit the correct keyboard keys.

We have had wonderful visits from family and friends. So many others have sent flowers, cards, and prayers. Thanks to everyone. Your thoughts, support, and prayers are very much appreciated.

Mary is being challenged, again. She was readmitted to the UCSF Medical Center today and is currently in the Intensive Care Unit at Moffitt Hospital. We haven't quite figured out what the problem really is, but the obvious symptoms are very low blood pressure and low oxygen content in her blood. On top of that, the x-rays show pneumonia in the left lung. Her sister Joyce is flying in tomorrow to be with her.

So, please keep her in your prayers and thoughts.

Thanks.

Tony

Friday, May 25, 2001 @ 10:09AM

Mary Update

Just a quick update. Mary is still in ICU. I get mixed signals from the staff there. On the positive side, her blood pressure is back up (actually high) without the BP meds. On the downside, it is taking more measures to keep her oxygenation up to acceptable levels. Last night they put her on a full face pressure mask. We are hoping she does not need to have an air tube inserted. Also, the cultures are not yet grown, so we don't yet know what has caused this pneumonia.

She is depressed and wondering how this will all turn out. Again, on the positive side, they were able to give her some anti-depression drugs yesterday and she spent some time actually sitting up on the edge of her bed for two hours. On the down side, she requested and saw a priest on Wednesday and received the Sacrament for the Sick. She also gave me very specific instructions about each of our kids and declared that I needed to remarry No Later Than one year to someone no younger than 40. So, she is lucid and cogent, frustrated and concerned, but wanting to come back and do all those things still undone. On the downside, she is concerned about her potential quality of life after recovery because of all the problems she was having seeing, walking, and just getting things done.

Please excuse me if I don't answer everyone directly. We really appreciate all the prayers and words of support. For your info, I read her every e-mail we receive and your support does help.

Gotta run. Thanks again.

Tony

Friday, May 25, 2001 @ 11:11PM

Mary on Friday

Well, it's the end of another day.

Mary's breathing was really labored today and it became more difficult as the day wore on. Last night, when her oxygenation numbers dropped, they put her in a full face mask that provided 100% oxygen and gave her Atavan to relax her. As the day progressed, it became obvious that she would wear herself out just breathing.

Finally, this afternoon, we decided the breathing tube was the way to go. On the up side, it does the breathing for her, it provides a vehicle for them to "scope" her lung to try to figure out what she has, and it allows them to add a feeding tube to give her some sustenance. On the downside, she is now heavily sedated and therefore cannot communicate and she is more susceptible to non-friendlies going directly through the tube to her lungs.

The docs suggested an answer to the mixed signals received up to now. It appears that the antibiotics are winning the war against the bacteria causing the pneumonia; that's why her blood pressure numbers, among others, have improved. The question has been why it has continually taken more effort to maintain her oxygenation levels. The answer is that the pneumonia has most likely injured or damaged the lung surface and only a prolonged period of time will fix that damage. So, she is not getting good lung surface back in a timely manner.

The docs are still optimistic that the pneumonia is reversible and Mary can recover, but she has a tough battle in front of her. The next several days are key.

Thanks again for all the thoughts, prayers, and kind words.

Enjoy.

Tony

Saturday, May 26, 2001 @ 11:00PM

Mary's Saturday

After the doctors inserted the breathing tube yesterday, the nurses were not able to add the feeding tube because Mary could/would not tolerate the intrusion, as reflected in falling blood pressure and oxygenation levels. There was concern about her nutrition since she had not eaten since Monday and had been working hard to breath most of the week. This afternoon, at 3:00PM, they were finally able to insert the feeding tube and begin a nutrient flow.

Two of the hospital staff who had been on 11 Long during Mary's bone marrow transplant in December 1998, now work in the ICU. Yesterday, one of them recognized the name and my face and asked about Mary. Today, I steered her to Mary's room and invited her to look. She came back out with a quizzical look on her face, apologizing that she could not place the face. I showed her a picture of Mary taken about three years ago that I carry in my wallet and her face lit up. Bottom line, to most of the world, Mary does not look the same. Her face is swollen from the prednisone; her paper thin skin is splotchy and abraded in many places from recent events; she has a breathing tube inserted through her mouth and a feeding tube through her nose; there is in central port in the left side of her neck, an IV to monitor blood gasses in her left foot, numerous IVs in her right arm, a Foley catheter draining body waste, a lead on her right index finger to measure and report blood oxygenation, and a soft boot on her right foot to keep it from turning in; stockings and inflatable sleeves on her legs to promote circulation.

There is a bank of IV stands with three IV pumps to the left of her bed, slowly emptying all the bags of antibiotics, anti-fungals, saline solutions, other medications, and liquid food into her body. Over her head is the ICU monitor tracking her vital signs and alarming when anything gets out of desired perimeters. To the right of the bed is the ventilator, which is now breathing for her to conserve her strength. I can understand the lady's confusion, but to me, Mary is still the same lady pictured in my wallet.

Mary asked me several weeks ago if I minded how she looked; she was concerned that she would not be attractive to me. I tried to explain that when I looked at her, I only see the same Mary I met and kissed for the first time at Cheryl's party, the same Mary that walked down the chapel aisle alongside of me and followed me around the world to be the best wife and mother she could be. I tried to explain that it must be that one's eyesight fails as we age and we see more with our mind's eye what we want to see. To me, she is still the most beautiful person in the world.

Physically, Mary is more comfortable now, than she has been in quite a while. Her numbers are stable, she is not in pain, and she is getting nutrition. She is in the right place for this particular time in her life; the doctors are super, the nurses supportive, and everyone understands her medical history. Since the cultures have not yet grown, we can't say for sure what type of pneumonia she has, but it looks like it's progress has at least slowed down. Her doctor described her condition as Adult Respiratory Distress Syndrome (ARDS), a situation in which her lungs have been injured and will now take some time to heal. The breathing and feeding tubes hopefully will give her that time. She is heavily sedated, so I cannot read her your cards and e-mails but, believe me, they are appreciated.

Thanks for caring.

Tony

Sunday, May 27, 2001 @ 10:40PM

Mary and ARDS

Adult Respiratory Syndrome (ARDS); it sounds simple enough. From earlier conversations with the doctors, I figured it was just a fancy name for the damage done to Mary's lungs by her pneumonia and it would simply take time for the injuries to heal. The nurse today shared with us just how serious the condition is. He indicated that UCSF is one of the only three hospitals in the country that use a very aggressive protocol intended to improve the patient's chances of recovery, which he said were about one in three nationwide. The internet source gives the recovery rate as under 50%.

Mary's Sunday was not as comfortable as her Saturday. As part of the ARDS protocol, the respirator is breathing for her at a rate of 32 times per minute (which is very rapid). But, her breathing appears more erratic and labored, going over 40 on a regular basis. The nurse explained that she is essentially hyperventilating at the 32 rate, thus purging her lungs of carbon dioxide. Reducing CO_2 levels trigger the brain to breathe faster, explaining the 40+ readings. So, her body is in effect fighting the machine and requires additional meds to relax her. Nothing is easy. We hopefully are in for the long haul.

Tony

Monday, May 28, 2001 @ 9:33PM

Of Rings and Other Things

Mary's clinical condition is slightly improved. She is maintaining good oxygenation with the ventilator delivering 50% oxygen at 28 breaths per minute. She looks more relaxed, but her arms and legs have swollen because of the poor circulation. The doctors on both the ICU and CRI teams are encouraging. They have identified the bacteria in her lungs and have the proper antibiotics working against it.

When Mary entered the hospital last Tuesday, she had only one request. She was very proud that she had never had her wedding band off her ring finger and she wanted to keep that record intact if possible. I overheard her nurse for the day telling someone else that Mary had worn that ring longer than she had been alive and that she would honor that request as long as possible. When I arrived today, the new day nurse apologized for something he wished he had not had to do; he gave me a jar with Mary's wedding band in it. It had been cut off and spread open, making it very to read the inscription, "AEM + MEK 6-12-65". It is the first time off her finger since I slipped it on almost 36 years ago. On her ring finger, in place of the gold band, was a ring of dried blood, showing where the ring had been…

Small things sometimes carry the largest meanings.

Mary told me later that when she first entered the hospital in December 1998 for her bone marrow transplant, she did not feel that she would leave alive. Can you imagine the courage it took to sit on the bed and take those tiny pills that would eventually kill her diseased marrow? The trust in those caring for her! That was the week before John arrived to donate her new marrow. Our worst nightmare was that something would happen to John before the donation. What faith and courage!

Then, the transplant itself, again, just a tiny IV line running from the bag of marrow to the central line in her chest. It was amazing to see the red marrow work its way down the line and then disappear inside of her. We felt like we were witnessing the gift of life; it was. She returned to work on July 1999.

The follow-up biopsy in August 1999 — again, simply a small sample obtained by a minor procedure — showed evidence of CML in her marrow. Graft verses host disease was induced to kill the disease and the effects became a minor inconvenience, not fatal, simply debilitating. We felt she was making progress; there was no sign of leukemia in any of the follow-up biopsies and we looked forward to spending our golden years together.

2001 has been a real challenge. Her suppressed immune system seemed to catch every tiny bug going around. When they reinserted a central line in February to help her fight the fungal pneumonia, it really hit me hard as an indication that her condition had regressed. Through all of her trials, however, she remained the model patient and maintained a positive attitude.

The small cut ring struck me hard today as well. I don't know what it means just yet.

Sorry about the rambling. Thanks for your thoughts and prayers.

Tony

Tuesday, May 29, 2001 @ 6:59PM

Tuesday in Nor Cal

Anybody else notice what a beautiful day it was in Northern California, today? Bright blue, cloudless skies, temperature in the 70's, slight breeze rippling over the bay, and cautious optimism about Mary.

Her numbers remained stable on this, her eighth day in ICU. But, they are staying up even when she is moved or jostled, unlike the last several days when BP, HR, and oxygenation numbers dropped dramatically in those situations. It tells the medical staff that her lungs are improving, a hypothesis supported by new x-rays. For the first time, the staff is mentioning that she may not have Adult Respiratory Distress Syndrome and that her lungs are actually clearing as the pneumonia is moved back. There was also talk of reducing the respirator function, to a point where it would no longer be breathing for her, but rather would support her breathing on her own. If she is able to do that, the next step is to remove the breathing tube. Wouldn't that be great? We should know in the next couple of days.

Some thoughts to live by:
- God never gives you more than you can handle.

- Reality exists in our minds. Each of us is unique and sees the world differently; what is important is our perception or read of the situation. We shape our existence.

- What happens to and around us in life is not nearly as important as our response to those circumstances. We alone are responsible for our behavior and reactions.

Having said that, I need to confess that I have been ambivalent about Mary's recovery from this ICU episode. From the beginning, my prayers have not been for her recovery, but rather for what is best for her. She has suffered a lot in the last 5 months or so, and she herself has questioned whether life in pain, with poor eyesight, hearing, manual dexterity, and mobility, is worth it. But, she has been the model patient, always working hard in therapy and conscientious with her meds, doing more than her share to return to normal life. It's now time to follow her lead. If she is successful in this latest battle, the doctors and I are going to have to figure out a way to energize her immune system without triggering debilitating levels of graft verse host disease to give her a chance to win the war. She cannot continue to be so susceptible to every bug in the air.

So, bring on the future! We're ready.

Oh, I figured out the significance of the cut wedding ring. It simply means that it was too small for her swollen finger. A local jeweler is enlarging it a couple of sizes and I will slip it back on her finger tomorrow while she is still sedated. She will truthfully be able to say that she has never knowingly had the ring off her hand.

Thanks for the prayers.

Tony

Wednesday, May 30, 2001 @ 9:17PM

Of Hometowns and Communities

Ever ask yourself what makes a hometown? Ten years ago, for the first time in our adult lives, Mary and I had the opportunity to decide for ourselves where we wanted to live. We took the month of August 1991 to drive from east coast to west, and finally decided, for a variety of reasons, that Fairfield was good or better than anyplace we had seen. A little over three-years later, we moved to Vacaville. Mary readily tells everyone she meets how much she loves this city and her life here. It's the simple things — a family doctor we trust, a church community we are comfortable with, neighbors who are friends, the weather, all the beauty nature provides here and close by, the library, the concerts in the park, and the people. The latest example — when I picked up Mary's wedding band at the jewelers this morning on the way to the hospital. They refused payment for putting it back together in the larger size. They were familiar with her story. So, thank you, Thornton's Jewelers on Merchant Street in Vacaville; I heartily recommend them to anyone who wants quality work done by super nice people. Mary is wearing her ring again!

Mary had a comfortable day. The doctors did cut back the respirator function at 6:30 this morning and she has done well breathing on her own, supported by the machine. Her P. E. E. P. (The over pressure the respirator maintains in her lungs to keep them from folding in on themselves) has been reduced from 10 to 8 and now, 5. They have reduced her sedative dosage (morphine and Versed) and are waiting for her to become reasonably alert before they pull the breathing tube. She has to be conscious enough to cough and clear her lungs on her own; so maybe later tonight or in the morning. Her rectal tube is gone, as her GI tract is now producing solid waste. There is now a sign on her door warning visitors of her neutropenic condition; this is a good thing as now, everyone will be aware of her immune suppressed condition and use the proper care. She is recovering and winning this battle.

Thanks again, for all the prayers and support. Unlike hometown, communities are self-made. You are Mary's support community and it is our job to generate the positive energy she needs to return to normal life. We are proud to have you as friends.

Tony

Thursday, May 31, 2001 @ 11:32PM

Of Small Victories and Perspective

At 2:19 this afternoon, Mary was lucid enough to have her breathing tube pulled. She was not fully conscious, but she was able to acknowledge my presence with a nod and to squeeze my hand on command. That was enough for the doctors to give the okay. The nurses warned that she would essentially have to learn to breath again, like a new born, and they were correct. Her exhalation was raspy and it was some time before she was comfortable, but her stats stayed good. The X-rays showed her lungs clearing, so hopefully the worst of this battle is behind her.

This is a major victory in a very small skirmish in this huge war she is fighting. But, I'm learning that you have to set very short-term goals and celebrate the victories along the way. As one friend said tonight, you climb mountains one small step at a time. This promises to be one long climb.

The medical teams are looking for stability in her cardiovascular and respiratory functions before they release her from ICU; that could be in a couple of days. She will most likely go next to the hematology-oncology ward on the 11th floor in Long Hospital before, I expect, transitioning to an acute rehab center, again. So, she is more than a few weeks away from coming home again and, even then, she most likely won't be any stronger than before her latest hospitalization episode. Her quality of life at that time was extremely poor and light years away from anything she might be comfortable with. I only share this information to put today's victory in perspective. But, hey, let's celebrate success in this step.

Some folks have asked me about visiting. Now that she is regaining consciousness, she probably would enjoy seeing friends. There are no promises about her stamina and, as of today, she still wasn't able to talk. They allow two visitors at a time (no children under 12 admitted). Please honor the neutropenic restrictions (no fresh flowers or fruit; wash your hands going in; and don't visit if you're sick). They clear the ward of all visitors during shift changes (7 - 8:30) both morning and evening, so target your visit before or after those times. She does not have access to a phone in the ICU.

Thank you all for the continuing support.

Tony

Friday, June 1, 2001 @ 11:03PM

Expectations and Reality

Mary (softly): "Tony, please help me."

Tony: "What can I do for you?"

Mary: "Help me stand up."

Tony: "Mary, you can't stand up. You're not strong enough."

Mary: "Yes, I am!"

Tony: "What do you want me to do, Mary?"

Mary: "I want to go home."

Tony: "I love you, dear."

Mary: "I love you, too."

From yesterday's progress, I expected Mary to be alert and interactive today. Instead, she moaned loudly with every exhalation, slipped in and out of sleep, looked through unfocused eyes, worked continually to get out of bed, and spoke only of wanting to leave. The staff called it "ICU psychosis" and said it was common among ICU patients. On the positive side, all her numbers are good and stable. She would have been cleared from ICU to a floor ward today, except for her mental state. They want her more aware of what is going on and capable of finding and pressing the Nurse Call button, if necessary. Right now, she requires more constant observation than she would get in a ward.

The learning today is not to expect linear progression; there are most likely unforeseen intermediate steps between even the seemingly closest waypoints. She is obviously physically better than yesterday, but much different from what I expected.

It really struck me how physically weak Mary is right now. Plus, it broke my heart to hear her plead with me to help her to do something that is just impossible for her right now. She is a fighter, with a very long campaign in front of her.

Thanks again for all the thoughts and prayers.

Tony

Saturday, June 2, 2001 @ 11:05PM

The Strength of Spirit

Early today, Mary was much like yesterday. But, as time progressed, her mind became clearer and her expressions more cognizant. Although her speech is very slow, soft, slurred, and often hard to understand, she is aware of what is going on around her and is speaking in full sentences. Although her vision is still miserable, she appears to be trying to focus, does recognize visitors, and does follow a person's image and speech. Even though there is not much emotion in her voice or on her face, her spirit is once again coming forward.

With her numbers still good and the sedatives finally wearing off, the staff agreed with her request when she once again asked to get up. It is no small task to transfer an ICU patient to a "neuro-chair," with all the monitoring cables, IV lines, and catheter lines attached to her body, but she transferred. More correctly, Mary's role was to lie still with her arms crossed as the staff lifted her from bed to chair. The neuro-chair is essentially a gurney whose shape can be reconfigured to that of a chair. That chair can be pushed anywhere within reason. So, Mary toured the ICU ward (all two bays) and then sat for some time in front of a big picture window facing the Golden Gate Bridge. She crunched away on crushed ice pellets, the first solid or liquid anything she has had in her mouth in almost two weeks. Her brother, John became her hero because he found the ice machine and kept her cup filled. I'm sure the beauty of the scenery was lost on her because of her vision problems, but I know she appreciated being out of her bed, the room and in the middle of a conversation with three other people (the third was her nurse).

Staff tells me there was a lot of luck in her rapid recovery — she came to the right hospital for her history and condition; she was admitted early enough to slow and stop the pneumonia before it did more damage; and the feeding tube went to the correct location the first time, providing her nutrients and strength to fight this disease (Thanks, UCSF/ICU nurses). I suspect it wasn't luck.

Mary's spirit continues to push the limits of what she should be able to do. There is obviously a larger Spirit looking over her, energized by all the prayers being offered in her name. There must be a lot more she is meant to teach us.

So, we are celebrating life one day at a time.

Thanks again,

Tony

Sunday, June 3, 2001 @ 11:49PM

If You Love Me

Mary: "Tony, don't put me through that again."

Tony: "Mary, you would have died without all this effort."

Mary: "Don't put me through that again."

Tony: "I have your medical power of attorney and I won't let you go that easily."

Mary: "We have to talk."

Concerned that I wouldn't honor her wishes, she summoned our youngest (Leslie) into the room and called our oldest (Jessi) by phone, repeated the message to them, and asked them to remind me of this conversation at the appropriate time in the future. To Leslie, she sang a few bars of "If you love me, let me go...."

With that business behind her, Mary proceeded to dazzle everyone today. She entertained Ron and Vicki in the morning, two more in the early afternoon and two more in the late afternoon. Even the hospital staff in two wards marveled at her sense of humor, perspective, and motivation to get better. On her 13th day of Intensive Care, she finally transferred to 11 Long, the Oncology ward. As unhappy as she was there during her most recent stay in March - April, she was exuberant on her arrival today. Not satisfied to just be there, she asked for something to eat and for help sitting up on the side of her bed. Those sound like small requests, but with her recent medical history and lack of physical strength, they were major feats and small victories to be celebrated. For the first time in a long time, she had no pain!

The future challenges are daunting. Her eyesight is shot and there are two of everything she does see. She has absolutely no muscle tone and little manual dexterity. She is so immune suppressed that they treat her as though she is neutropenic. That said, her spirit soared today.

Mary's frustration before this latest adventure was that she has not been able to do all that she once could. With her current challenges, it will be a long time before she is again, "whole". Today, I suggested to her that the Lord had a reason for bringing her back one more time. In earlier discussions, she had mentioned that she wanted to be remembered as a life-long educator. Though we can never know for sure, I offered that perhaps she is meant to share her thoughts with the world and that we should co-author a book. I asked her to begin to think of ideas; thankfully, she liked the idea and it was rewarded with a big smile. If we pursue this, she will have a mission and purpose, which she can achieve and succeed at, that will not be impacted by poor eyesight, mobility, or dexterity. If this endeavor makes sense to you, please help by reminding us of anecdotes or instances where Mary had a positive impact. I'm not sure how this will all come together just yet, but Mary has touched so many lives positively that I would like to begin documenting her approach and techniques. Your thoughts are welcome.

Mary is now in Long Hospital at the UCSF Medical Center. She has a phone next to her bed. Her phone number is (415) XXX-XXXX. She may have trouble answering the phone because her vision and dexterity problems, but be assured that, by today's behavior, she served notice that she is ready to work hard to improve her capabilities and return home.

Thanks so much for all the support and prayers.

Tony

Monday, June 4, 2001 @ 11:04PM

Holding Her Own

It's been a remarkable day. Mary is much like
yesterday, mentally alert and active, but physically weak.
She missed more phone calls than she took today
because it is difficult for her to see and hold the phone.
She is eating "thick liquids" — things like apple sauce,
milk shakes, and iced tea so, hopefully, she can lose the
feeding tube sometime soon. She is so weak that she
cannot roll over by herself, but she is eager to start PT
and OT to build her strength. Her attitude and
approach puts a smile on the face of everyone she meets.

As quick and sharp as she is, she occasionally sees or
imagines things that are not there; simple things, like the
penguin we left in the ICU room or books on the shelf.
Small price to pay to see her so pain free and alert.

PAIN FREE — that's the key. For the first time in
months, she is pain free. The sky's the limit if she can
remain this way.

Surprise guests arrived tonight. My mother and two
sisters showed up at the house. Talk about welcome
visitors. I am so glad they are here and Mary is eager to
see them tomorrow.

No news is good news, right now.

Thanks for the support and prayers.

Tony

Tuesday, June 5, 2001 @ 11:56PM

Of Mind and Matter

From the moment we arrived, Mary pushed to shine. She immediately asked to get out of bed. With help, she transferred from the bed to a chair and held court with my mom and two sisters, sharing gossip, recipes, and war stories. Back in bed for a rest afterwards, she requested pizza, salad, and an ice tea from the cafeteria. Amazingly, since the only solid food she has had in the last two weeks was some apple sauce last night. Then, she requested a wheel chair, to which she again transferred with help. With IV pole and oxygen bottle in tow, she toured the entire ward and then settled into the solarium for more female talk and a jigsaw puzzle. By the time she returned to her room, she was exhausted and needed help from the lift team to get back into bed. Tired but proud of herself, she called it a day and bid us adieu.

Physically, there is much good news but plenty of challenges. On the positive side, they stopped the flow through the feeding tube and will pull it if she shows she can take enough nutrition through her mouth. (Hopefully, the sausage and pepperoni pizza will agree with her gut). Her platelet count is rising and her skin bruising is beginning to clear. She received her last IV dose of antibiotic and was given some hand exercises by

Occupational Therapy to begin to restore her manual dexterity. She continues to be pain free! On the down side, Mary's body is essentially a mass of soft tissue, with no muscle tone and little strength. Her eyesight is extremely poor and I'm not convinced it can all be blamed on her glaucoma; the UCSF team is planning on having their eye experts look at her while she is there. Her blood pressure is still high, but that is way down on the staff's list of concerns. She is connected to a Foley catheter and has no control of her bowel movements.

That said, the plan is to move her to an acute rehab facility on Friday if they have bed space. We would prefer some place in Sacramento or Solano, but our PCP is committed to the Laurel Grove Hospital in Castro Valley. We could change PCPs to find one who would recommend something closer, but we respect Dr. G too much and want to stay with him. If that is the right place for her, that is where she will go.

Mentally, Mary is sharp, alert, and entertaining about 85-90% of the time. The rest of the time she tends to forget where she is. She told my sisters today she would make tuna casserole for dinner tonight and a cheesecake for dessert. Tomorrow, she plans to visit several antique shops in Vacaville with them. When I called her from home tonight, she asked three separate times when I would be home for dinner and told me to drive safely.

Her drive to perform is commendable, but almost seems too extreme. Dr. L referred to it as a manic response.

I should be excited about her progress and motivation, but I have this uneasy feeling deep inside. Make no mistake, I am extremely proud of all she has done to date.

Perhaps, it has to do with her mental state. She has been through a bunch the last three years, but I never felt like she wouldn't be there tomorrow. Even during her recent stay in ICU, when she could have easily given up, I never felt deep down that she would not pull through. But, when she lost her mental capacity for two days during her hospitalization in early April, I was crushed. It's possible to live with physical problems, but her mental problems hurt. At that time, I truly thought we had lost her and I grieved.

Thanks for the thoughts and prayers.

Tony

Wednesday, June 6, 2001 @ 10:21PM

Leslie's Words

Leslie visited Mary at UCSF today and I did not, so
I will ask her to share her thoughts with you. - Tony

Today, I drove to UCSF with my son, and family
friends, Pearl and Mark. It's been wonderful to have so
many people offering to visit mom these past weeks and
it sure makes the drive a lot easier with company
(especially when my son thinks that it is time to cry
whenever we start driving over the Bay Bridge). Mom
was sleeping when we arrived in her room. To look at
her, she looks like she is twenty years younger than last
week. As she was sleeping, I noticed how calm her
breathing was and how great her skin looked. While in
the ICU, the doctors put an extra amount of holes in
her arms and even in her legs which seemed to bruise
over and become very dark. In the last days, her bruising
is getting lighter and many of her sores are actually
healing before our eyes. After a little massage of her feet,
mom woke up and smiled at us. She said she felt great
but was tired.

When we went back into her room after giving her
time to sleep, we kept telling her how great she looked
and she said that she was "healing from the inside". I
told her that if that's the case then her insides must look

wonderful because her outside looked beautiful. Her sense of humor is better than I ever remember my mom's being. I brought her a bag of chocolate chip cookies made by my husband and she said that we could have a PART of a cookie because she wasn't sharing. I told her I make her cookies all the time and she said that she likes Casey's better.

Mom received a big, beautiful bouquet of balloons from her niece, Anne. Anne wrote that my mom promised to dance in her wedding and she was going to hold her to that promise.

My parent's 36th wedding anniversary is this month and I can only hope that any of us can feel the strength that they seem to feed off each other during these tough times and use that to hold our own loved ones and let them know how much we care.

Good night.
Les

Thursday, June 7, 2001 @ 10:35PM

I Believe!

This lady is amazing. Mary's progress since Tuesday surprised me today. She can roll over by herself. Her skin splotches are dissipating and her abrasion wounds are healing. She held court sitting in a chair for over an hour and actually ate her cottage cheese and fruit plate for lunch. Her eyesight and manual dexterity are still poor, but she was able to operate the television set at her bedside. She compiled a list of places in San Francisco she thought my sisters and mom should see and sent us on our way early. She built a request list of clothes and other things she will need at the rehab facility. Her throat is still sore, but her voice was definitely less raspy by the end of the day. She claims to be healing from the inside out and getting better every day, and now, I believe!

On the caution side, she still has the feeding tube and Foley catheter installed. She is not even close to being able to support her own weight standing and she has little control of her bowels. Knowing her starting point, however, simply reminds us of how far she has come and how far she still has to go. Prayer works!

The game plan is to move her by ambulance to the Laurel Grove Hospital at the Eden Medical Center in

Castro Valley tomorrow, Friday, in the late morning. This is the same facility she was at April 12-27 after the last discharge from UCSF. They require a minimum of three hours of aggressive rehab daily, so she should be pushed there. Their mission is to teach people how to be relatively independent again, by showing them how to move without injuring themselves, transfer to the walker and wheelchair, eat, dress, get about, and use the bathroom on their own. She appreciated the positive atmosphere and support there in April, so she is looking forward to the challenge. My sisters and mom leave tomorrow. We will join Mary at Laurel Grove and send them on their way from there. I will pass along Mary's new address and phone number when she finally settles in there. My guess is that she will probably be there at least three weeks.

So, keep the thoughts and prayers coming. They are appreciated.

Tony

Friday, June 8, 2001 @ 11:43PM

Life is Precious!

Mary transferred to the acute rehab facility today, a little later than expected, but she is there. She continues her phenomenal progress. Before she left UCSF, they removed her IV central line and feeding tube. She still has the Foley catheter, though it would not be a stretch to expect them to remove it tomorrow. She is on supplemental oxygen as a precaution following her bout with pneumonia. Her voice is returning to normal, her mind is straight, she devoured half of a roasted chicken for dinner, used the commode for the first time in weeks, and toured the facility in her wheelchair. Her spirit is great and she is looking forward to her next hair wash and massage. It will probably take 2 - 3 weeks for her to regain enough strength and independence to return home.

One thought comes to mind as Mary continues to recover. How precious life is! Her fight back only confirms the value and potential of every minute every day. Life is such a fragile gift; it is a shame to waste any of it. Mary's passion has been to see the good in every child she meets and to encourage each to develop his or her potentially.

How many lives did you touch positively today?

Keep the prayers and comments coming.

Thanks.
Tony

Saturday, June 9, 2001 @ 11:02PM

She's Untethered!

Mary's last support line — her Foley catheter — came out today! She continues to eat most of the food put in front of her and can help support her weight on her leg when the nurses transport her to the wheelchair or portable commode. She is totally lucid and, for whatever reason, composed and serene. Without pain, she appears more relaxed, content, and motivated than she has in a long time. Who is this woman? My heroine!

On the challenge side, her right foot drop has some of the doctors concerned; they plan to bring a neurologist in to look at it. Her eyesight is still grim, but she has been cleared for cataract surgery when she gets home again. Her manual dexterity is poor, and PT/OT are working with her. Her physical strength is minimal, but she is prepared to work on it. The staff warned her not to expect linear progress, but rather some regression after every advance. Sort of two steps forward and one step backwards as a general pattern.

Mary's recent experience has reinforced one big lesson for us. This is a serious consideration. Illnesses and threats to health sneak up on us. Everyone needs a game plan for the worst case scenario. Some questions to consider:

Does anyone else know which bills to pay and how you pay them?

Where are your important papers?

Who plays the role of Tony for your Mary?

How far do you want medical science to go to keep you alive?

Do you have a durable power of attorney for healthcare decisions?

Have you discussed final arrangements — cremation or burial, final resting place?

Do you have a will and/or trust?

Is there anything special in your estate that you want to go to a particular person?

Have your children been brought into the discussion?

These are not pleasant topics, but it is important that they be asked, addressed, and answered.

Please feel free to call or visit Mary. She does appreciate your support and would be thrilled to speak with each and every one of you.

Tony

Sunday, June 10, 2001 @ 10:20PM

An End and A Beginning

Mary is still in great spirits and eating voraciously. Her body is obviously healing. She eagerly anticipates your e-mails and appreciates all your prayers and support. She begins her first full day of PT and OT tomorrow at Laurel Grove.

Having said that, this will be the last daily update on her condition, unless there are significant changes.

My intent was always to ensure that Mary's friends would not be surprised if she did not pull through. Now that she is beyond that stage, she begins the long process of rehabilitating her body. It promises to be a lengthy, though not very dramatic, journey.

Thank you for all the positive feedback and supportive comments. Please keep in touch by e-mail, phone, snail mail, or personal visits. Your support means everything to both of us and we'll need it over the long haul.

Tony

Thursday, June 14, 2001 @ 11:19PM

Daffodils and Other Lessons of Life

Mary finished her first week at Laurel Grove today. On the positive side, she still has no pain, she is eating regular foods, and can, with minimum help, transfer from bed to wheelchair and back. Wearing a brace to support her "drop foot," she can walk a short distance with a walker. On the downside, she still has very little physical strength or stamina, she has poor manual dexterity, and her vision is worthless beyond a distance of about six inches.

The game plan for her future is coming together:

- Eden Hospital did an MRI of her spine yesterday to attempt to identify the cause of her drop foot.

- The Laurel Grove staff's plan has her staying there until June 28th; our health plan insurer has neither approved nor disapproved that request just yet.

- When she is discharged from Laurel Grove, depending on her capabilities, she will either go to a skilled nursing facility or come home. Even when she eventually comes home, she will need help 24 hours a day, seven days a week. That means finding a nursing service to help provide that care.

- I'm told that the ophthalmologists have cleared her for cataract surgery. If this is true and the cataracts are confirmed to be the cause of her vision loss, we should be able to schedule the procedures for sometime after she gets home.

- My challenge, before she comes home, will be to prep the house for Mary's return. That means having the house scrubbed, cleaning out the air conditioning system and the vents, and cleaning the carpets.

- Mary's job is to show she is physically and mentally capable of participating in, and continuing day after day, the three hours of PT and OT daily, as well as improving on a schedule required by the health plan insurer. Her attitude is super; the question is whether her physical structure is sturdy enough.

Flowers have always been important symbols in our life together, particularly roses and daisies. A friend sent us the following story about daffodils that carries a key lesson for life. [The Daffodils story — attached]

Thanks for all the prayers, phone calls, cards, e-mails, and flowers. Continue to plant your daffodils.

Enjoy life.
Tony

The Daffodil Principle
By: Margi Harrell

Several times my daughter had telephoned to say... "Mother, you must come see the daffodils before they are over." I wanted to go, but it was a two-hour drive from Laguna to Lake Arrowhead. "I will come next Tuesday, " I promised, a little reluctantly, on her third call.

Next Tuesday downed cold and rainy. Still, I had promised, and so I drove there. When I finally walked into Carolyn's house, and hugged and greeted my grandchildren, I said,"Forget the daffodils, Carolyn! The road is invisible in the clouds and fog, and there is nothing in the world except you and these children that I want to see bad enough to drive another inch!"

My daughter smiled calmly, "We drive in this all the time, Mother." "Well, you won't get me back on the road until it clears — and then I'm heading for home!" I assured her.

"I was hoping you'd take me over to the garage to pick up my car. How far will we have to drive?"

"Just a few blocks," Carolyn said, "I'll drive. I'm used to this."

After several minutes I had to ask, "Where are we going? This isn't the way to the garage!"

"We're going to my garage the long way," Carolyn smiled, "by way of the daffodils."

"Carolyn," I said sternly, "please turn around."

"It's all right, Mother, I promise, you will never forgive yourself if you miss this experience."

After about twenty minutes we turned onto a small gravel road and saw a small church. On the far side of the church, I saw a hand-lettered sign, "Daffodil Garden."

We got out of the car and each took a child's hand, and I followed Carolyn down the path. Then we turned a corner of the path, and I looked up and gasped. Before me lay the most glorious sight. It looked as though someone had taken a great vat of gold and poured it down over the mountain peak and slopes. The flowers were planted in majestic, swirling patterns, great ribbons and swaths of deep orange, white, lemon yellow, salmon pink, saffron, and butter yellow. Each different-colored variety was planted as a group so that it swirled and flowers like its own river with its own unique hue. Five acres of flowers.

"But, who has done this?" I asked Carolyn.

"It's just one woman" Carolyn answered. "She lives on the property. That's her home."

Carolyn pointed to a well-kept A-frame house that looked small and modest in the midst of all that glory.

We walked up to the house. On the patio we saw a poster.

"Answers to the Questions I Know You Are Asking" was the headline. The first answer was a simple one. "50,000 bulbs," it read.

The second answer was, "One day at a time, by one woman. Two hands, two feet, and very little brain."

The third answer was, "Began in 1958."

There it was. The Daffodil Principle.

For me that moment was a life-changing experience. I thought of this woman who, I had never met, who, more than thirty-five years before, had begun — one bulb at a time — to bring her vision of beauty and joy to an obscure mountain top.

Still, just planting one bulb at a time, year after year, had changed the world. This unknown woman had forever changed the world in which she lived. She had created something of ineffable magnificence, beauty, and inspiration.

The principle her daffodil garden taught is one of the greatest principles of celebration: learning to move toward our goals and desires one step at a time — often just one baby-step at a time — learning to love the doing, learning to use the accumulation of time.

When we multiply tiny pieces of time with small increments of daily effort, we too will find we can accomplish magnificent things.

We can change the world.

"It makes me sad in a way," I admitted to Carolyn. "What might I have accomplished if I had thought of a wonderful goal thirty-five years ago and had worked away at it 'one bulb at a time' through all those years. Just think what I might have been able to achieve!"

My daughter summed up the message of the day in her direct way. "Start tomorrow," she said. "It's so pointless to think of the lost hours of yesterdays. The way to make learning a lesson a celebration instead of a cause for regret is to only ask, "How can I put this to use today?"

Saturday, June 16, 2001 @ 12:16AM

Mary's Field Trip

Westmed Ambulance Dispatch (by phone): "Mr. Mras, your wife went into respiratory distress this afternoon as we were transporting her from UCSF back to Laurel Grove. Her blood pressure became very elevated and her respiratory shallow. We left her at the Emergency Room at the Summit Medical Center in Oakland."

Tony, "Oh, no! How do I get there?"

We had spent a comfortable day at the UCSF Ambulatory Care Center where Mary receives her follow-on oncology care. The last time the staff there had seen her was May 22, when they had called the paramedics and sent her to the ER. Most, honestly, probably never expected to see her alive again. Yet, here she was, back for another appointment, physically weak but with food numbers and a positive spirit. She did not want this appointment, as it would preempt her rehab work at Laurel Grove, but she had decided that, if she had to go, she would enjoy the experience. She shined for Dr. L, her nurse and all the staff. We learned that her cataracts are mild and probably not the cause of her poor vision; therefore, that surgery is not likely to help much. Her graft-verses-host symptoms have lightened to the point they felt comfortable reducing her prednisone dose from 15 to 10 mg per day. She received her third monthly infusion of a special drug to counter her osteoporosis. After confirming that the ambulance was on its way to pick her up, I left for Laurel Grove to beat the traffic.

What could have gone wrong? Not only was she making progress physically at the rehab center, but she had regained her interest in reading and crossword puzzles. Despite not being able to see details beyond 6 - 9 inches or to manipulate a pencil smoothly, she was now telling me about newspaper articles and doing my crosswords. Although her weight was down due to her reduced muscle mass, she was eating voraciously. Her swelling was gone and her skin was clearing. How could she relapse so quickly? Could I find the place and get there in time?

Summit Security Guard: "I'm sorry, sir. The nurses say no visitors."

Tony: "Listen, after all we have gone through together recently, my wife is not going to die alone in there. Let me in."

Imagine my surprise and relief when I saw Mary lying comfortably on a gurney in the hallway, disgruntled and hungry, but no worse off than when I left her at UCSF. The ER nurse explained that Mary should never have been dropped off there; it was simply a case of an inexperienced ambulance crew being overly cautious about Mary's stats. What is normal or acceptable for Mary right now, because of her medical history, would be dangerous for others. Concerned, the crew erred on the side of caution and diverted to the nearest emergency room.

As we sat side by side on the gurney, holding hands, waiting for the ambulance to return, we both decided that the one thing we missed most during the latest phase of Mary's great adventure is the opportunity to lie next to each other in bed, holding hands, and listening to each other breathe. A little more than 7 hours after requesting the ambulance pickup at UCSF, Mary finally completed the 30 mile trip to Laurel Grove and dove into a dinner the staff had set aside for her.

Prayer works. Thanks for the comments and support.

Tony

Monday, June 18, 2001 @ 12:30AM

This Special Day

Mary reviewed the previous e-mail updates and reported there was one glaring mistake. In my life after Mary, I was to remarry NET (not earlier than) one year later, not NLT as previously reported; something about not rushing into things. Our oldest daughter, Jessi, questioned the minimum age of 40; saying, "Dad, that's not much older than me." Jessi, in life, chronological age is a lot less relevant than attitude. With that said, we can now celebrate Mary's continued recovery.

Mary's physical capabilities remain limited, but her mental outlook is super. Although her eyesight seemed even poorer today, she read the Sunday newspaper and did the crosswords. On the other hand, from a distance of three feet, she mistook a pillow for another patient's amputated leg; sorry, Betty. Her manual dexterity is a little better — she can turn the pages of the newspapers, as long as she wears latex gloves. She added notes to several cards, took numerous phone calls, and even briefly played piano. She even placed a couple of outgoing calls using a pre-paid calling card. Today, was day one of her reduced 10 mg prednisone dosage.

Today, was also Sassy's first birthday. I believe that the puppy is important to Mary because it represents everything she thinks she is not right now.

Sassy is young, healthy, energetic, strong, independent, enthusiastic, agile, and athletic, with her whole life in front of her. Hopefully, Mary will have many more years of better health to continue to bond with and teach Sassy.

Today was also Father's Day. Mary's comment was that making me a father was her pleasure. My mom's comment was that her eight children are her jewels. Our three children — Jessi, Mike, and Leslie — are precious to us; I cannot imagine life without family. We are so proud of them and the responsible adults they have become.

So, today was special. But, then, every day is special. Hopefully, the joy and strength of your families made your day today.

Enjoy.

Tony

Wednesday, June 20, 2001 @ 11:25PM

Frustration

Mary: "Tony, I can't do any more. What do they want of me?"

Tony: "Mary, it has nothing to do with your attitude or effort. You cannot do any more than what you are doing."

Mary was as despondent as I had ever seen her since her early days in ICU. The case manager at Laurel Grove had just shared with us that Health Net has challenged the appropriateness of the acute rehab facility for Mary's condition. Her poor structural support, strength, and stamina had made this a question before her discharge from the UCSF and her uneven progress since then has highlighted the issue. She has given her all; the concern is that she is not strong enough to make the required weekly progress. The alternative is a less expensive convalescent home/skilled nursing facility that would require only one to one and half hours a day of PT/OT and a less aggressive improvement schedule.

On the up side, Mary has made considerable progress at Laurel Grove. She is now able to stand from a sitting position, she has a tremendous appetite, and she continues to take more control of her world. On the downside, her eyesight is still abysmal and her drop foot is still a factor.

That this will be a long slow recovery process is now very evident. At times, we get impatient. "Lord, please give us our lives back." But, then, we recognize that it does no good to focus on the things that we cannot control and which we can no longer do. Mary can only do what she is physically able to do. We have to focus on the opportunity each day brings, do whatever each of us can do, and celebrate every victory, regardless of how minor. Plant one daffodil bulb per day and rejoice in the joy and beauty of life and nature, for as long as we have the gift of life. I believe the Lord's Will be done, as long as we do our part. That's why, with the California Super Lotto at $90 million, I bought a lottery ticket today. We probably won't win, but there is absolutely no way we will, even if the Lord wants us to win, unless we do our part and buy a ticket.

It looks like Mary may transfer from Laurel Grove to a skilled nursing facility before the 28th. The positive of this development is the opportunity to have her closer to home in Vacaville. She would get to visit with her puppy and family/friends would have easier access. With less time on the road and out of the house, our lives would become more normal. We will see.

Thanks again for the feedback, prayers, and comments.

Keep in touch.

Tony

Saturday, June 23, 2001 @ 11:15PM

Serenity

"Tony, I can't do this. You have to read to me."

Mary had asked me to bring a magnifying glass from home to help her see. Now, she had received a personal letter from friends and had carefully maneuvered her wheelchair to several places in the room to get the best light. Even with the paper 4 inches from her eyes and the magnifying glass somewhere in between, she had given up the effort.

"Tony, would you consider me blind?"
"You probably are legally blind right now, Mary."
"I'm so frustrated!"

This is a lady who has loved books all of our married life, and has devoured them since her transplant. Her reading list numbers 36 in 1999, 71 in 2000, and 8 in 2001 (all before this cycle of hospitalizations). Now she only sees gradations of light and dark. She identifies visitors by their voice. Several years ago, she went totally deaf in her left ear, so locating sources of sounds is also difficult, adding to her frustration.

We had assumed her poor vision before this latest phase was a result of her graft-verse-host disease. She has had several visits with a local ophthalmologist and was recently examined by the UCSF ophthalmologist; no one seems to be able to tell us why her eyes have deteriorated so rapidly. They agree that her cataracts are still mild, so their removal would not help much. She uses several different eyedrops — lubricating drops for dryness, antibiotic drops for infection, and Timoptic for glaucoma. Her next appointment for her eyes is scheduled for July 5th.

She is still in Laurel Grove. Our health plan has offered a skilled nursing facility (SNF) in Vallejo; we request Vacaville. They said, if it's Vacaville you want, SNF "A" is our place. We responded that there is no way she will go there; we want her to go to SNF "B". So, that negotiation continues. Mary will most likely move early next week, maybe Monday or Tuesday.

Except for her eyesight, she continues to grow physically stronger each day. Although she'd not sturdy enough to stand up and transfer (to walker, wheelchair, or commode) independently, she can do it on her own (supervision is required to ensure she does it correctly and is caught in case she falls). She has been measured for a brace for her "drop foot" and hopes to receive it Monday. Her weight is up 4 pounds since her arrival at Laurel Grove, so all that eating is having an effect. Her attitude remains superb, so we continue our daily baby steps to physical recovery.

One benefit of sharing thoughts is that people share back. That feedback puts things in perspective. Two friends need to be added to your prayer list — one whose ovarian cancer has returned after eight years and another whose leukemia has stopped responding to treatment. God's Will, dignity, and serenity are the three things I ask for people in situations like theirs and Mary's.

That said, another friend suggested this prayer:
God grant me the serenity to accept the things I cannot change, the courage to change the things I can, and the wisdom to know the difference.

Living one day at a time; enjoying one moment at a time; accepting hardships as the pathway to peace.

Taking, as He did, this sinful world as it is, not as I would have it. Trusting that He will make all things right if I surrender to His Will; that I may be reasonably happy in this life, and supremely happy with Him forever in the next.

Thanks for the continuing support.

Tony

Monday, June 25, 2001 @ 11:47PM

Knowledge is Power

There is a sculpture in the Air Garden at the Air Force Academy that carried the motto, "Knowledge Is Power". Not to be confused with that other saying, "A little knowledge is a dangerous thing". Either way, knowledge offers explanations and generates solutions.

Because of her recent near loss of vision, Laurel Grove sent Mary to a local ophthalmologist this afternoon. Dr. E did a very thorough evaluation and covered all the bases. Her retinas, pupils, and optic nerves are in great shape. She does not have macular degeneration. She does have significant cataracts, though they are not the big problem right now. Her eye pressure is normal. What she does have is a major problem with her corneas. Spelled phonetically, he said she has "filamentary carotitis," also called, "epifilial defects," which are caused by dryness and abrasions to the cornea. The initial fix is simple, just an adjustment to her eye drop regimen. He stopped the Timoptic (he indicated it could cause dryness) and the antibiotic (she doesn't have an infection). He changed her lubrication drops to different ones that don't include a preservative. Hopefully, her vision will begin to return soon, as that is her biggest handicap right now. One prayer answered.

On a different front, we have not heard from our health plan about Mary's next move. Each day she is at Laurel Grove, she gets stronger and more capable, so we are not complaining. The original target date was June 28th, and that's Thursday.

The custom brace to correct her drop foot was delivered today but, as built, maintained her improper foot angle instead of correcting it; Wednesday is the target date for the revised model.

One day at a time.

Tony

Thursday, June 28, 2001 @ 11:41AM

Mary on the Move

Just heard from the case manager at Laurel Grove.
Mary is cleared to come home tomorrow, Friday, June
29.

It's probably a result of two factors.

- First, she has worked hard and has been making
  super progress. She is not as far along as she was
  the last time she left Laurel Grove and is not
  cleared for independent transfers, but she is
  standing and walking comfortably with a walker
  on her new foot/ankle brace.

- Our health plan has been unable to find a skilled
  nursing facility willing to take her for the
  standard daily rate, once they see the cost of her
  daily medications.

Because of her continuing challenges, she will need
someone around 24/7 and home health care will be
required for some time. Her eyesight is slightly better
this morning, so hopefully the diagnosis is correct and
the treatment is working. With tomorrow's sunrise, we
move on to the next phase of our life together.

Speaking of challenges needing continued prayer,
Mary's cousin's wife is scheduled for triple bypass

surgery today. We pray the Lord gives her the strength to come through this day better than before.

Enjoy.

Tony

Friday, July 6, 2001 @ 8:11PM

Decisions

"Whee! This is fun! Tony, I feel empowered!" Mary had just had her brace adjusted so that it does not cut into her calf and was now zipping around Raley's Super market in a battery powered shopping cart. Smiles are truly contagious. By the time we left the store, this blind, grinning, speeding bumper car driver had nearly everyone in the store laughing along with her because of her obvious joy.

"Tony, you're a long distance man. Where does a girl find one of those today?" asked Patricia one of Mary's nurses when she was in ICU at UCSF last month, when she learned we had been married 36 years. "Love is a decision," I answered. "Choose your love and then love your choice". Shared values and attitudes are much more important to a long term compatibility than common activities or backgrounds. One day at a time, one small step at a time, and it's suddenly 36 years later.

The good news is that Mary is home. The bad news is that she needs continuous attention. Home care nurses in the area get $20 per hour, which approximates $40,000 per year. I would need to earn about $60,000 per year, before taxes, to just break even on home care costs. I need a joint work business plan that allows me to work out of the house most of the time.

It is not what happens to a person in life that is important; it is that person's response to the challenge that is key. In our society, we tend to think of success in financial terms. However, we play so many different roles at one time and success is actually measured in each role. Focusing on the failure areas can be frustrating — income generation, National Foundation for the Teaching of Entrepreneurs (NFTE) establishment, Certified Financial Planner (CFP) certification, service at church — from any perspective, performance has been abysmal. But, supporting Mary in her battle has been a real joy.

The lesson — we control our destiny through the force of our will. The old story about glass being half full or half empty — our perspective tempers our view of the world and plays heavily into our decisions. How we look at things generates our response and impacts on all those around us. We decide to enjoy; we decide to love; we decide to reorganize; we decide the priorities in our life; we choose our mate; we decide to be optimistic.

Mary visited the ophthalmologist yesterday and ordered a pair of glasses. The best she can hope for is probably 20/100 vision, but that is better than her present situation. The ophthalmologist also agreed to remove her cataracts, if her oncologist will clear her for surgery. So, perhaps, her vision will improve. Char gave her a bottle of water from Lourdes, which Mary has been using on her drop foot, and she is regaining control of the foot. She can stand, dress, transfer, and even cook by herself. Her doses of immune suppressants are down and her mouth ulcers are minimal. As she told me the other night, she has decided that this time she will beat all the things currently challenging her.

Yes, she is home again and working hard. Thanks for all the prayers, thoughts, and positive comments.

Tony

Tuesday, July 17, 2001 @ 11:36PM

What Does it Mean?

"What does it mean, Cheryl?" Mary asked her nurse practitioner at UCSF, with tears welling in her eyes.

"Please don't send me to the hospital. I don't want to go back into the hospital."

Mary's chest x-ray at her monthly visit to UCSF today showed fluid in her lungs, and Cheryl had diagnosed bacterial pneumonia. Cheryl simply responded that Mary had an infection she had to get beyond, that we caught it very early in the cycle, and she would not have to be hospitalized at this time. There are three more pills added to her daily medication diet.

Mary's progress has been phenomenal since her return home two weeks ago. Her PT and OT trainers have consistently described her as an over-achiever, and she had made great strides physically. She navigates well with her walker and wheelchair, and actually pictures herself walking across the room (until she catches herself). Her modified brace works very well and she has pretty much recovered her drop foot. She picked up a pair of glasses from her ophthalmologist yesterday and, for the first time in a long time, could see more than gradations of light and dark. The cataract surgery is on hold until her health improves, but she can now at least see the television screen with her new glasses. She dresses herself and does most of the cooking. Her skin is still fragile and splotchy, but it looks better. For the first time in a while, her legs today were not very swollen. Her steroid dosage is down and her graft-verse-host disease impact (other than her skin) is better than it has been in years. So, what does this diagnosis of pneumonia mean?

With four hospitalizations this year already, we had decided something had to be done to increase our odds and change the pattern. The HVAC ducts, the carpets, and the house have all been professionally cleaned since Mary's recent return home. What will it take to keep her well? What does it mean?

With the Lord's help, this simply means that Mary's recovery will not be consistent and linear. Her spirits are still superb. Except for a raspy cough, a shortage of breath, and three additional pills each day, she is the same hard charger impatiently working toward her return to good health.

Thanks for the thoughts and prayers.

Tony

Monday, September 17, 2001 @ 9:55AM

Resizing the Ring

"Tony, it's beautiful! Do you like it?" Mary was trying on her newly resized wedding band at Thornton's Jewelers and was excited about the results. Her original ring had been cut off in ICU several months ago and Thornton's had enlarged it to fit her swollen fingers. Now, her arms and hands are extremely thin and Thornton's had resized it again, adding a second band next to the first to give the original more strength and durability. It seems that 36 years of constant use had worn the original thin.

After 4 hospitalizations in the first 5 months of 2001, Mary had resolved she would not return to the hospital. Air duct cleaning, house scrub down, and carpet cleaning accompanied her most recent homecoming in June. The plan appeared to be working.

Her pain was gone. She regained muscle tone in her legs and has been able to move about using her walker or wheelchair. As recently as last week, she would show off her improving strength and balance by walking across the room without any support. Despite poor eyesight, she started reading again, going after whatever books the local library had in large print. With a strong appetite, she insisted on making gourmet meals and desserts for me, family, and friends. She has been able to get to Saturday Mass and communion, and even attended a special healing service. Our follow-up visits to the clinic at UCSF are now monthly instead of weekly.

For all the progress she has made, she faces major challenges each day. Her eyesight is shot, with severe cataracts being the principle culprit and filamentary karontitis taking the care of the rest. She is a candidate for cataract surgery, but only after she is well enough that it is not a life threatening procedure for her. Her skin is paper thin and tears easily; the wounds that result from any abrasion take forever to heal. She bruises easily, as evidenced by purple blotches all over her arms and neck. Her stomach is distended and her arms and hands are extremely thin. Her lower legs and feet are swollen and weep constantly, leaving pools of water wherever she goes. But, through all this, she has a smile on her face and readily tells anyone who asks that she is doing just great.

Yesterday, her right foot and calf turned bright red and were hot to the touch. By the time she arrived at the emergency room at UCSF, the redness had moved up her leg to her hip and across her stomach. Early diagnosis is a fast moving skin infection that they immediately began treating with 3 different antibiotics while taking cultures to figure out exactly what it is. When I left her early this morning, they had three separate IVs going, plus a Foley catheter, had moved her to Intensive Care, and were putting in a central line in her groin to be able to put more volume into her.

Since then, the plan this morning is to give her two units of blood due to low hematocrit. She is also receiving dopamine to keep her blood pressure up; it tends to drop with heavy duty infections. The redness has started receding from her abdomen, so the antibiotics are working.

It has been an interesting week for a variety of reasons. On the grand scale, America is once again at war. On a personal level, Mary is back in ICU.

One day at a time.
Tony

Monday, September 17, 2001 @ 10:33PM

Sepsis and Cellulitis

"I'm sorry Mr. Mras, but you cannot go into Mary's room right now. We just had an event."

I had just arrived at the UCSF and was told it would be about 15 minutes before I could go in to see Mary. Even when I was allowed into the area. Mary's bed was surrounded by 10 to 15 staff at any one time, all working hard to diagnose her condition and improve her chances of survival.

Her heart rate had changed dramatically, her blood pressure had dropped to 60 over 30, her respiration was raspy, her platelet count was down to 22, her oxygenation level was falling, and she had become unresponsive. Finally, after several hours of work and massive infusions of antibiotics, fluids, platelets, and "presser" drugs, as well as oxygen under pressure, her vital signs stabilized and she rested.

What is going on?

The skin infection, which they thought could be "cellulitis," has begun to recede and her right leg has lost its bright red color. Her major problem is a serious blood infection they are calling "sepsis," against which they are using the correct antibiotic. There is concern about her heart, but a sonogram did not show any obvious problems. There is also concern that her leg problems may have been caused by a blood clot, although the sonogram could not find one. We are looking for her vitals to stay stable as they reduce the infusions of the presser drugs (which increase blood pressure by constricting blood vessels and increasing heart rate).

The challenge, one more time, will be to maintain her respiratory capability long enough for the antibiotics to defeat the infections. Once again, we are having the discussion about possible use of a breathing tube and ventilator, if it comes to that.

She received the Sacrament of Extreme Unction again today.

Joyce, her sister, is coming in from Kansas City tomorrow to spend some time with her.

Thanks for the prayers and support.

Tony

Monday, September 17, 2001 @ 10:55PM

Change Notice

Just got a call from the hospital. Mary has taken a turn for the worse and they asked that I be there with her. Leslie will pick me up and we'll spend the night with Mary.

God's Will be done.

Tony

Tuesday, September 18, 2001 @ 8:31AM

Getting Closer

By the time Leslie, Casey, and I arrived at the UCSF ICU, it was already after midnight. The staff had intubated Mary at about 9:30 Monday night, and the ventilator was now breathing for her. They had maxed out the doses of the three "presser" medications and her blood pressure was once again acceptable. Her liver tests had shown abnormalities and she was not producing urine, but she was once again stable and comfortable, though gravely ill. At 3:00AM, we left for home.

The 5:30AM phone call this morning reported that her heart had stopped and that the staff had restarted it with medications. The 6:30AM phone call confirmed that her liver and kidneys were not functioning properly and requested inputs about how far we wanted to go to bring Mary back from the next expected episode.

The 8:30AM report indicated that her kidneys were still not functioning and her liver was worse. I've called the immediate family and I'm heading back to the hospital.

Mary told me several times recently that she feared death, but she could not explain why. I shared with her that, to me, death is not something to fear, but rather a release from pain and suffering and simply the final chapter in our life story. My fear is that we will not have done enough with the time and talents God has given us to leave the world a better place.

Perhaps a premonition, but on the day prior to her current hospitalization, Mary and I cleaned and organized the kitchen. One of her jobs was to reduce the stack of CDs to those she wanted out and I put the rest away. Last night, as I wandered around the kitchen, I noticed that she had left one CD by itself on the top of the rack; in big letters across the front was the name REQUIEM.

God's Will be done.

Tony

Tuesday, September 18, 2001 @ 6:15PM

FINALE

AAAAAARRRRRGGGGGGGGHHHHHHHHH HHH......

Mary passed away at 2:05PM, PDT, today. Services will be this weekend, date and time to be determined.

Mary's struggle is finally over; she is at peace.

The finality of it all is just starting to settle in.

Enjoy each other.

Tony

Thursday, September 20, 2001 @ 1:06PM

FINALE

Thanks to everyone for the prayers and words of support. Many of you have asked about service.

<u>Visitation/Rosary:</u> Sunday evening, September 23, 2001, from 5:00 - 8:00PM.

<u>Funeral:</u> Monday morning, September 24, 2001, at 10:00AM at St. Mary's Catholic Church.

<u>Reception:</u> Immediately following the funeral at Mary's home.

If you are traveling from out of town to attend, please let me know in advance as many of the neighbors have volunteers bed space in their homes.

In lieu of flowers, Mary would appreciate contributions to the Leukemia Society of America or to one of her two favorite charities: Food for the Poor and Habitat for Humanity.

Peace.

Tony

Epilogue

After saying goodbye to Mary — my mentor, my mother-in-law and my friend — I promised myself to live my life as she had done, unabashed and fearless. I found immediately that what she did effortlessly, was actually quite difficult. I set small goals each day to accomplish. With my husband deployed to fight the War on Terrorism, I was alone in Warner Robins, Georgia with our children. Lucky for us, my mother's family resided in nearby Atlanta, and I made great friends in our neighborhood. I relied heavily on their support and encouragement to push through my sadness of Mary's passing.

Adapting Mary's attitude towards life helped me keep my house clean, my vegetable garden thriving and my family fed with healthy beautiful meals for at least a year. I practiced hard and trained for my Black Belt in Taekwando, became amazingly fit and completed my Bachelors degree in Marketing Management. These were huge accomplishments for me. Mary would be proud.

The problem with living a life of intentionality, is that life gets in the way if you aren't careful. When the children became more involved with school sports and Girl Scouts, it became harder to keep my personal goals consistently at the top of the list. Basically, I was a busy mother of two and I got distracted. I allowed one thing after another to replace the items on my goal sheet. The only thing I managed to maintain was my avid reading list — one book to broaden my mind, and the other for pure entertainment.

Keep learning. Keep your mind active.

As the years passed, I'm ashamed to admit that I forgot my promise. Michael accepted a new military assignment at a base in Colorado. As we made arrangements for our move, I found a home that Mary would have absolutely loved. She had always advised to buy more house than you can afford, and although we spent more than we ever had, we stayed within budget.

Buy more house than you can afford.
Doing so will keep you striving forward to keep it comfortably.

I felt empty after our move to our new home. My sisters and mother lived within an hour's drive away and I made new, wonderful friends, but it wasn't enough. My talks with Mary were sorely missed. There were so many times I reached to the phone to call her and ended up crying because she wasn't there anymore.

I began a new list of things to accomplish. What would Mary advise me to do to get out of my slump? My inner Mary suggested that I work on my brain. Although I wasn't working, I should work on being employable, so back to school was the decision. My Master's degree in Quality Systems Management was completed in one year. I began working for a local Benefit Auction company raising funds for non-profit organizations. Then, began volunteering with Grace Be Unto You Outreach Ministry to help with those less fortunate in our community. I joined a speaking group called Toastmasters International to improve my ability to communicate. Even with all these outside interests, I still felt empty. More years passed and I felt as if this, being busy yet still feeling empty, may be my new state of being.

I started at yet another school called the Leadership Program of the Rockies hoping to help me find my place in this world; something to help me feel complete. I wanted to help make our community a better place for my children and the future. After graduation, I became very active in local politics and for years I thrived in this endeavor.

On May 21, 2014, I was working on several documents on my computer: two political papers, balancing the outreach church checking account, researching doctoral programs and catching up on emails. I was interrupted by the alarm on my phone. It was time to pick up our children from their high school. I was exhausted and miserable. I put my head on my desk for a moment.

"God, what am I supposed to do? I'm so tired. Please help me decide," I cried out loud.

I had to stop this pity party, I had to get moving. I cleaned up my face and jumped into my car to head towards the school. My favorite music CD by Natalie Cole was playing and I cranked it louder to sing along. At the top of my lungs, I sang my stressors away. I turned onto the main drive of the school when — WHAM! — My life flashed before my eyes when another car came out in front of me and we collided.

When I woke up, I learned that my car was totaled and that my children were with me, scared for my well-being. I was on the ground leaning on the side of the car. I was shaken, but fine. My husband arrived and retrieved me from the ambulance to bring me to the Emergency room. I was physically fine, just bruised and in a lot of pain. After a few hours, the Emergency Room released me with a mild concussion, medicated my pain away and sent me home. I slept well for the next few days. In my bouts of lucidity, I was in physical agony. I muscled through the pain and restarted my regularly scheduled activities with my eldest daughter as my chauffeur.

At twelve days post accident, I was at the bank depositing a check when the teller looked at me with a quizzical look.

"She does this a lot since her car accident," my daughter responded to the teller's confused expression.

"What do you mean?" I said, "I'd like to deposit this with cash back."

"Mom, it's okay," said my daughter with her hand rubbing my back, "My mom would like to deposit this check with some cash back."

"That's what I said." I responded getting a bit agitated.

"Mom, you said, macaroni cheese spaghetti. It's okay, you're just tired." My daughter attempted to comfort me.

The teller shook her head in agreement and completed our transaction. My daughter brought me home all the while explaining to me that I had been speaking nonsense words and my pattern was getting worse.

That day was a huge surprise to me and the first of many bad days. Soon, I was unable to truly communicate. My brain was working, but the words wouldn't come out of my mouth correctly. I tried writing, but the written words were as scrambled as the spoken ones. I was articulate yet trapped in my mind.

My misery was intense. I had gone from performing multiple tasks and having a sharp memory, to being unable to complete one task and not remembering the words that had just left my mouth. Depression set in deep. What good am I? What did I do to deserve this? Why take my ability to communicate in all forms? Why? I sat in my house crying and wallowing in self pity.

The next thing I knew, I heard a voice inside my head. It was Mary's voice saying, "Get up. You're not dead, yet!" I smiled.

She's right - I'm not dead. I got up realizing that I still had my brain, I still was me. The glass is refillable. I had to fight to regain my ability to articulate.

"I will find and fulfill my purpose for living through this accident," I told myself.

During my cognizant periods, I made arrangements to be evaluated by my doctor and fought to find the source of my brain issues. I thought my fits of rage, paranoia and confusion were a result of my frustration of not being able to communicate nor be alone for long periods of time. Eventually, the tests showed I didn't just have a concussion, but a traumatic brain injury (TBI).

You don't know what to do?
Figure it out.

Now, that I knew the cause of my memory lapses, I could go through extensive treatments to recover and reroute the injured portions of my brain. Since then, I have come a long way through my recovery and have accepted my new normal by finding ways to work around the things my brain no longer will do.

I'm okay. Why? Because, I have implemented my 'Mary mode'. I take time to enjoy everyday by "eating dessert first". Simply enjoying each moment I'm allowed, starts my day in a positive mindset. I've purged negativity from my life. Yes, that includes negative people. Not until my brain injury did I realize how much dealing with negativity drains me. The experience of removing negativity is freeing.

I have a plan for my future and have goals to actively pursue it. Everyday beings another opportunity to fulfill my dreams and encourage others. I've learned to enjoy the journey in addition to reaching the destination.

It took a brain injury for me to finally be at peace with who I am, who I'm meant to be, and to finally, Eat, Drink, and Be (like) Mary.

Words of Wisdom

Adventure

Mary would purposefully get lost in order to find new areas. She would take turns at random while driving home. At worst, she would have to backtrack to where she started.

Mary loved a bargain.
She never hesitated to stop at a Garage Sale, Thrift Shop or Antique dealer.

Children

"Ya'll hush" — was her gentle discipline for her class room.

Mary loved children. She would always take the time to smile and talk to children. She believed children just want to be noticed. Smile, get them to smile back, and you've made the experience better for the child and the caregiver.

Once I was with Mary when she began a conversation with a new mother with her baby. Mary looked at the baby, and in the sweetest voice exclaimed, "Your baby has your eyes!"
Later, she admitted she had nothing else nice to say about the baby.

When out with her adult children, people would remark that she looked too young to have adult children. She'd reply, "They're Tony's children from his first marriage". Conveniently neglecting that she is his first wife.

When friends brag about their super star children, Mary would say, "Ours are delightfully normal".
It took the pressure off the children and they honestly received praise and support when they excelled.

Mary never lied. She just didn't tell the whole truth.

While grocery shopping with her children, her rule was if they went to the store and helped, they each could choose one item for a dollar as a reward.

Mary walked fast. If her children didn't keep up while shopping, she simply would page them before she walked out.

As they grew, they walked faster than she did, and she'd complain for them to slow down.

Read out loud to children, and animate throughout. Bring the book to life.

She said, if you don't want your kids to play in the street, send them out without shoes.
The street is hot.

Mary never let her grandchildren win at tic-tac-toe.

When a dear friend became estranged from her son because of his choice in bride, Mary persuaded her to reconcile with the argument that she would want to be involved with the future grandchildren.

Confidence

Tony was concerned about an upcoming flight evaluation. As an instructor/examiner pilot, Tony didn't have a lot of hands on flight time and he worried his flying proficiency could suffer. Mary was non-plussed; her response, "If you aren't good enough to pass a check ride, I don't want you flying".

Don't doubt yourself. She encouraged that if you don't know how to do something, "Go figure it out". It usually worked — eventually.

Mary was most comfortable when in charge.

While living in Arizona, Mary would often skinny dip in the pool they had in their backyard. Although the family had a tall fence around the backyard, Mary would use the diving board which brought her well above the fence line.
Tony was amazed there weren't more car wrecks near their intersection.

Education

Mary was a voracious reader.
Always read two books at a time, one trashy and one educational.

Never stop learning.

Visit your local library.

She had no time for people who weren't willing to learn.

Mary taught at private schools to offset her children's education. Once they moved into high school/college, she taught at public schools. She felt the purples needed her more.

Mary once confessed that she disliked teaching at private schools because many of the parents refused to admit their children were anything but perfect.

Mary stressed the importance of education. When her children dreamed of fantasy careers, she advised, they can do anything they want after they received their education.

Three rules for college: She and Tony would pay for the first four years of college. They will pay each class once. If they married before they graduated, they were on their own.

Mary and Tony offered a car at graduation to any child that went to a service academy.

Food

If you can read, you can cook.

Always try new food.

Cook by color and you'll always have a nutritious meal.

Always eat dinner as a family. Turn off all distractions. One child helped cook, then the other two would do the dishes.

Take a smaller portion of food than you want. You can always get seconds.

Taste twice before you season your food.

Each child could pick one food they never had to eat. Everything else was fair game.

When in doubt, make a casserole.

Mary enjoyed creating gourmet dishes for the family. She could make a meal out of whatever was in the pantry and refrigerator.

She once used the cookie jar to make pickled cow tongue.
No one ever ate cookies from the jar again.

Fashion

Mary loved bright clothing and large obnoxious jewelry.

After reading, "As An Old Woman, I Shall Wear Purple", Mary declared, "Forget that, I'm going to wear purple now!"

Mary had been dying her hair for so long, she claimed she had no idea what her natural color was.

Friendships

Mary never had a large group of friends. She always had a small, but close group.

Mary spoke to everyone like a friend.

There are too many people in your life to allow one to bring you down.

Music

Mary loved loud happy singing, even if the singer couldn't
carry a tune.

Enjoyed Broadway musicals especially Little Shop of Horrors.

Learn the piano or guitar so you can play and sing.

Perspective

As Tony and Mary walked through a mall one day, they were approached by a group of rough looking male teenagers, with sagging pants a gang-like feel about them. Tony began to steer Mary away from the approaching group when a big smile cam across her face and the leader responded with a loud, "Hello, Mrs. Mras." As a middle school principal, she had established a positive relationship with these young guys. Sometimes, you have to get past appearances to see the real person.

When asked about the boys with the sagging pants, she responded with, "It is easier to catch someone running away from mischief if the crotch of his pants is near his knees and he needs one hand on the waistband to keep the pants up".

Relationships

Think before you speak. Words spoken can never be unsaid.

Always have your own checking account.

Don't get married until you can comfortably take care of yourself.

Wait to have children. Get to know each other as a married couple, first.
When your children grow up and leave you need to know you can tolerate each other.

Never stop dating.

Don't get a king sized bed. A couple should be able to touch. On a king, you may as well be alone.

Never go to bed angry.

Words and actions speak volumes. Mary thought through everything. Not that she wasn't spontaneous. She was always aware of the impact her words and actions had on others.

Family should never intentionally live apart. During the Vietnam War Tony was sent to fly out of Taiwan. Mary worked to earn the airfare and took the family to Taiwan so Tony would be able to come home each night.

Work

Always be employable. Even if you never work, always be
ready to work in case you need to.
Keep up with school requirements and all credentials.

Dress for the job you want, not the one you have.

Mary was results oriented.
When she decided that Tony's tennis and yard work
took up too much time on the weekends for them to
spend quality time together, she hired someone to do
the yard work, then had Tony pay for the service.

Take naps whenever possible. She took a nap everyday
after school. It helped her think clearer. She forced her
children to nap as well. They quickly learned that the
naps were fro mom and they didn't need to sleep, but
merely be quiet and remain in their rooms.

Life in General

Whenever you find yourself in a pattern, break it.

The only difference between a rut and a grave are the
dimensions

— Ellen Glasgow